MUSINGS OF A MIDDLE CLASS MIND

RANDOM THOUGHTS ON THIS AND THAT

RISHI GROVER

Made with ♥ on the Notion Press Platform
www.notionpress.com

I express my intense gratitude to my wife Ritu, my daughters, Nidhi & Shubhi, and my parents, for motivating and tolerating me.

Contents

Contents

Preface

I always wanted to be a writer, i.e. after I had stopped wanting to join the army, become a movie director, a professor, a pilot and finally, a gangster. The other professions owe me a collective vote of thanks, for not joining them.

In the meanwhile, largely due to an innate interest in the Biological Sciences and partly due to a pathological hatred of Maths, I joined Medical College. From the first year itself, we had to write so much in our exams that I was afraid that God had redirected my application to the wrong department for approval.

After years of ghostwriting FB posts for others on various days like Women's Day, Daughter's Day, This Day, That Day etc (but never being acknowledged by anyone), SAT essays for many lazy kids and grocery lists for my wife, one day, my friend Abhishek Laddha, motivated me to start blogging and introduced me to Medium.com.

The ball was thus set rolling. Some readers liked what I had written and these few messages of appreciation went straight to my head. I ended up dreaming of becoming the next J.K. Rowling overnight. Except for the fact that I lack her imagination, look nothing like her and write nothing like her. Another interesting fact is that I look exactly nothing like George Clooney either.

So here we are, with a collection of my writings, a few of which have been posted as blogs previously. It's an eclectic mix of topics, ranging from train journeys, vacations, and mid-life crises to my aversion to spicy food. Those who have stayed in hostels in the 90s, especially in government-run colleges, may easily relate to the references to hostel mess food.

I couldn't think of a sequence to put them in. Should I put the serious ones together or the travel ones or maybe the ones on college life? I prayed to God for some divine guidance, but I think He must have been on vacation and there was no help from that quarter. So I have just put them randomly in no particular sequence.

I enjoyed writing each and every one of them.

If they make you smile even once, my aim is achieved.

CHAPTER ONE

TO BE AN INDIAN

What does it mean to be an Indian? India is a huge country. More than being huge, it is very diverse. The Gujju or Marwadi at one end is as different from the Manipuri or Arunachali as the Kashmiri is from a Malayali. While we all identify as Indians, we are also identified by typical characteristics which often define us.

The typical Delhi-wala is constantly portrayed as a brash fellow who keeps asking people if they know who his father is. One instantly imagines a tall-ish, jacketed fellow on a bike or in a car, breaking rules all around and asking everyone around "Tu jaanta hai mera baap kaun hai?". People automatically assume that he is a conceited brat, but giving him the benefit of the doubt, isn't it possible that he may just be a simple, naive soul looking for his lost father?

The moment one mentions Haryana, the image of a tall, well-built, wrestler type with a wooden stick (latth) in hand comes to mind. I visited Gurgaon recently. Sorry! Gurugram! I had to go to Gurugram recently to attend a conference. Just to be safe, I had carried a sturdy helmet with me to prevent serious injury if any of these fellows bashed me on the head with a latth just for fun. I was surprised that Gurugram is full of swanky high rises and malls and high-end hotels and normal-looking people. I looked around but could not see the hordes of brawny oafs running around beating up people. I felt quite safe but the helmet felt quite offended at not being used.

The other day, I had lunch with a Rajasthani friend. After the meal, when he offered to pay, I asked if he was feeling alright because Marwaris are supposed to be very kanjoos (miserly) businessmen. He was actually an IT professional in a multinational and settled abroad. But his knowledge of Hindi cuss words and exotic descriptions of assorted parts of the human anatomy was impressive.

Two decades ago, before my first trip to Vellore, which is located deep in Tamil Nadu, I had been warned by many friends to be careful. "Tamilians don't like North Indians", "They are very rude to Hindi speakers" "They will misguide you" and so forth. Once in Vellore, I had to go from the main hospital to Bagayam, where the Medical College building was situated. I asked a traffic policeman at a crossing "Sir! Bagayam?" He signaled me to wait and then continued with his business. I was just beginning to feel offended when he made a bus stop in the middle of the road. Then he motioned me to get on to the bus and said "Sir! Bagayam!" Not only was I not misled or mistreated, but this gentleman went out of the way to stop a bus for me at the intersection and made me board it there itself! All preconceived notions went for a toss. And I felt like a fool, a North Indian fool!

For North Indians, South India means dark-skinned Madrasis, idli, dosa, sambhar, lungis and a gibberish language in which you say Aiyyo Aiyyo frequently. As far as the North is concerned, there are 3 main areas in South India: Chennai, Bangalore and Hyderabad, the geographical locations of which are vague. There is also some city or town called Kerala, which is forever on strike. That there are separate states with different cuisines and languages, is a concept which many North fellows find difficult to grasp. Or maybe they don't want to.

But the knife cuts both ways. For the South Indian, everything north of the Vidhyas is North India. And North Indians are a semi-cultured, loud and often uncouth breed. And they speak Hindi which is a very very difficult language; a statement which we simple-minded North Indians find perplexing because Hindi is easy; it is Tamil and Malayalam and Telugu which are difficult!

There is more to this than meets the eye, The Gujjus are offended at being clubbed together in the same category as Uttar Pradesh (UP) or Bihar, which they feel are poor, underdeveloped, crime-infested areas which provide cheap labour to the rest of the country. A Gujju would rather migrate to Burkina Faso than be compared to a UP 'bhaiya'. Which is actually quite derogatory to the UP and Bihar guys, most of whom are simple and very hard-working fellows. And some of these poor chaps also go to Mumbai to be abused and beaten up, now and then, by some or the other Sena.

Mumbai, the city which never sleeps, where the dabbawalas win hands down against Swiggy and Zomato, where people spend half their lives slogging to pay the rent and the other half commuting in local trains, where the white-collar South Indian works shoulder to shoulder with the D'Souzas and the Patils. Mumbai is the city which the Mumbaikar doesn't want to leave (except on weekends) and where nobody from the rest of India wants to stay.

But there is another place where everyone wants to go: Goa. In the rest of India, Goa is stereotyped as the land of beaches, which is full of easy-going guys, who are constantly drinking feni and partying and making merry at joints run by the Russian mafia.

It's not difficult being a foreigner in India. But sometimes it is tough being an Indian in India. And no one knows that better than the North East dwellers. Firstly, most Indians have a very vague idea of the part of the country which lies to the east of Bangladesh. They will be hard-pressed to tell you the number of states, let alone their names. Even when they go to study or work elsewhere in the country, the North East dwellers are derogatorily called Chinese or Chinkies and it is believed that they eat dogs and the women are 'easy'. The poor chaps are treated (or should I say mistreated) as foreigners in their own country.

The Kashmiris also often get the short end of the stick. The Kashmiri Pandits were already uprooted in the early 90s and settled across the country. But the Kashmiris who go to the rest of India nowadays are also often looked upon with suspicion. People actually expect that they will suddenly shout Pakistan Zindabad and then try to sell you their carpets or apples. Come on guys! They are also honest fellows like you and me, trying to study or earn a living, away from their homes.

On the other hand, their neighbours, the Himachal Pradesh fellows are generally perceived to be simple, honest, silent and gentle hill people. This is the province where the Dalai Lama lives and is mostly remembered only during the summers when most of the rest of the country becomes an oven.

Himachal Pradesh adjoins Uttarakhand which is the hilly, benign and non-violent part which separated from Uttar Pradesh long back. Uttarakhand has Rishikesh, a place where people go to find inspiration to live. It also has Hardwar, the dream destination for dying according to Hindu lore.

Their other neighbours, the Punjabis couldn't be perceived more differently. Any mention of a Sardarji throws up an image of a jolly Sikh who enjoys his butter chicken and whiskey and has at least one family member in the army. There is a common misconception that Punjabis start doing the Bhangra for no reason at all. We do need a reason, any reason, even a very little reason to dance and make merry!

The Bengalis are the exact opposite and are considered to be steeped in culture with a sincere interest in the fine arts. At the same time, they are fond of their 'adda' and they love to argue over jhalmuri and puchkas. Bengalis are also odd guys because they enjoy football as much as, or even more than crickct, something which the rest of India (other than Goa and Kerala) find difficult to understand.

While Sikkim is mostly a national picnic spot, most Indians are also fuzzy about the region consisting of Orissa, Chhattisgarh and Jharkhand. They have a general idea that these areas are very poor, they have a lot of minerals and something called Naxalism happens here. Other than that, these are states which do not appear on any tourist guide.

The state which does market itself very innovatively as a tourist destination is Madhya Pradesh (MP). MP, known for its quirky tourism ads is also synonymous with pohe and jalebi and the lilting dialect of its people.

All said and done, India is a mishmash of colours, languages, cuisines, religions, geography and beliefs. In spite of all their differences, Indians are bound by their love for cricket and their general disregard for rules and regulations. We may not look alike, sound alike, speak alike or even think alike, but that is what makes us what we are today as a nation.

And finally, what does it mean to be an Indian?

Well, it means that we are equally comfortable cursing Westerners (who give us the cold shoulder abroad) as we are racially abusing Blacks and even some of our own fellow citizens.

It means that the North Indian can derogatorily refer to South Indian food as idli dosa but also be in awe of their cultural roots and their intellectual prowess.

It means that though we may not be able to locate Manipur on the map, we celebrate Mary Kom's Olympic medal with the same elan as a Haryanvi wrestler's.

It also means that we may become all patriotic with a single medal in the Olympics but still watch cricket till our eyes bleed and also try to see that our kids focus on studies and not on sports.

It also means that while we may become all dreamy-eyed on Republic Day and Independence Day and hoist the Tricolor with pride, most of us do dream of sending our children abroad.

It means praising the way people follow rules abroad, like in Singapore or Dubai but obstinately refusing to do the same ourselves, here in India.

Indians are a study in contradictions.

Happy but complaining.

Suspicious but honest.

Rich but frugal.

Nosey but helpful.

Flawed but lovable!

CHAPTER TWO

AND YET, I EXIST!

I am not on FB.

Or Twitter.

Or Instagram.

And yet, I exist.

Not only do I exist, but I live happily. As happily as a married man with two kids can.

One day, in 2006, my better half came and informed me that our marriage was in jeopardy. I was not on Facebook, hence I did not exist and it was difficult explaining to people that she was married to a non-existent person. The fact that we had a daughter, who existed, was unexplainable. To save our marriage, she went and created an FB account for me. For the password, she selected the name of the first medicine which came to her mind. Till today, my FB password is the name of a Gynec drug. I never got around to using my FB account.

After many years, suddenly I was notified by Facebook that my status had changed and that I was now wedded to my wife. Apparently, the Missus had put my status as single initially and many years later she went and updated my status as married and finally, we were an FB-certified couple! Needless to say, our online friends found this very funny and there were many congratulations posted (of which I learnt from all the email notifications FB kept sending because I still did not access my account)!

FB was mostly about people posting dull details about their breakfast, lunch, dinner, their bowel movements and their cat's food preferences. All done for 'likes' from faceless strangers. Who, in turn, expected you to like the nonsense which they post. The next Nobel prize is reserved for the person who invents an online toilet, where all the excrement you pass will be posted on FB in real-time. It will avoid the hassle of logging on and wasting so much time in posting garbage manually. So many man-hours will be saved; precious time which can be spent abusing others on Twitter or WhatsApp.

But now, FB is passé! Now, FB is the new Orkut. Only the oldies use FB. This generation is the Insta-Gen. My daughters are scared that I may open an Insta account and start following them. Worse, I may like their posts or post a Dad joke or a stupid 'uncool' comment and embarrass them online. They need not worry. I have no intention of creating an Insta account. Some pouting selfies which I have seen posted there, have given me nightmares. They looked like famine victims whose souls were being sucked out of their mouths. Also, I have no interest in seeing people's hairy feet or food which looks like something a dog has vomited. Garbage remains garbage, whether posted on FB or on Insta. Apparently, Instagram also has something called a 'reel' which is basically a way to demonstrate your stupidity to the world as a short video clip. If there remains any doubt about your IQ after reading your posts, the reels will reconfirm your status as a moron.

Along with Insta came the era of Twitter. Twitter users are technically 'twits'. For those who still don't get it, you could either Google the meaning of twit or consider reading Roald Dahl's classic story "The Twits". Twitter forced people to express themselves in 140 alphabets. All the chaps who loved to wax eloquent on FB were now forced to compress their infinite wisdom into 140 characters! And Twitter also gave a free hand to democracy and freedom of speech and expression; a brand of democracy which wasn't so welcome and a freedom we could probably do without. Any idiot with a smartphone could sign up on Twitter and publicly abuse the President of America for not speaking in Hindi or educate the public on how Ethiopia's budget would affect the Indian stock market.

And FB, Insta and Twitter were all full of narcissists who loved to post about their exploits. In the medical field, it was mostly someone boasting about the number of patients seen in one day, the number of surgeries performed, some fancy equipment purchased, some rare surgery performed (along with the patient's photo - his or her privacy be damned), a lecture delivered at the Kitty Party Organisers Association's Weekly Meeting and so on.

As if Twitter wasn't enough, we got WhatsApp. WhatsApp allows one to make closed groups, post nonsense among like-minded (or rather, equally mindless) people and discuss anything and everything under the sun. It liberates the 'Baba' hidden inside many of us. The Baba appears in the morning, posts a Good Morning message with a photo of a flower, sunrise, God or Ratan Tata, with a random inspirational quote and then disappears till the next day. Sometimes, if the self-styled motivator is busy in the morning, the Good Morning message is sent in the evening. The best thing about these messages is that nobody reads them, but everyone forwards them to other groups and people to try and spread 'positivity'.

Whatsapp is also the place for wishing people. Someone will post a message in the morning "Happy Birthday Rahul" and everyone who opens the group will keep wishing Rahul Kumar a happy birthday till Rahul Kumar says that it is not his birthday but actually Rahul Singh's birthday. Then everyone will wish Rahul Singh, till someone reminds everyone that Rahul Singh is not even in the group, because he is in jail for stabbing a Whatsapp group admin who wished him twice, on someone else's anniversary.

WhatsApp also allows people to disagree with others publicly on anything and everything. And there's nothing better than a fight where you can curse and abuse without any risk of getting hurt. From Kashmir to Kanyakumari and from Afghanistan to Burma (both are part of Akhand Bharat, in case you are wondering why...) we are a people who love to argue and force our beliefs upon others, whether it is politics, religion or food.

Also, on WhatsApp, everyone is an expert in everything, from birdwatching to the nation's economic policies to politics. Add to this a heavy dose of intolerance, disguised as patriotism and voila: a 5-star troll is ready! On budget day, we are economists. On China and Pakistan, we are defence analysts; during Covid, we were doctors but at the end of the day on the Housing Society Groups we go back to being bigoted idiots.

Not for me, this intense need to express my views to strangers or the hunger for likes or followers. I am not cut out for the nitty gritty of online verbal spats with faceless strangers on Nigeria's foreign policy or the existence of the microchip in the 2000 rupee notes. Neither am I comfortable with posting ostentatious lovey-dovey and mushy messages for my wife or kids on social media or boasting about my mediocre surgical skills. I also understand that people may not be interested in the bland oatmeal I had for breakfast or the colour of what I passed later.

I would rather exist peacefully offline.

Have chai with a friend.

Relax with a good book.

As we would say in Gujarat: Majja ni life!

CHAPTER THREE

A FEW GOOD MEN

The deadly second wave of Covid was in full sway and I had just returned from the funeral of a friend's father. As much as I would like to say that I had helped arrange it, I hadn't.

My friend's (let's call him JP) parents were struck with Covid on a visit to Silvassa. He was quarantined with the same in Mumbai. His mother passed away and he was ridden with guilt that he hadn't been there at the end or for the last rites. After this his father's condition worsened and the family was under even more duress. I managed to arrange a bed for him in a good Covid hospital in Surat (which was just a few hours' drive from Silvassa) and he was shifted here. His condition was significantly improved when JP reached Surat, after 6 days. Unfortunately, there were acute complications over a few hours and in spite of great efforts by the medical team, he could not be saved.

None of the family had ever set foot in Surat previously and since they were here solely on my suggestion, I too, was weighed down by guilt at the adverse outcome and the sudden turn of events. But we still had to get done with the formalities and the last rites. The hospital was extremely cooperative and despite the late hour, the formalities were finished quickly.

My friend is a Malayali, Roman Catholic and I had no idea of their rituals or where or how the last rites could be conducted. The first person I could think of was Susamma Sister, a senior Malayali nurse in one of the hospitals I visited. After the mandatory apologies for calling so late in the night, I explained the situation to her: a stranded family, a Covid victim and the need for a Catholic burial. She was extremely cooperative and suggested that I call one Mr. Saji at Kerala Samajam Surat and also asked me to call in case any help from her was required, irrespective of the time of day or night.

Reluctantly I called up Saji around midnight and explained the situation to him. He sounded brusque initially but on understanding the circumstances he mellowed down and wished to speak to a family member. Once a distraught JP was free in between calls to relatives, I had him call and speak to Saji. The subsequent dialogue was in Malayalam but I could make out that apparently nothing could be done in the middle of the night and we would have to wait out the night. But he promised to do everything in the morning. Which he did and how! I had to make a few phone calls to arrange for space in the Medical College mortuary (the private hospitals would not accept a Covid-positive body) and Saji promised to meet us there in the morning.

What followed next was nothing short of amazing. The coffin had already been ordered and reached the morgue on time. Thereafter, Saji reached there with his team and took over. The staff/volunteers at the morgue were extremely cooperative and helpful (and from all faiths, if I may add) and Saji had not only ordered the coffin but also got the flowers, some fragrant spray, a white sheet, candles, agarbattis and even gloves and sanitiser. We realised later that he had also arranged for a priest and for the grave to be dug and ready by the time we reached.

Once the body was released, they shifted it to the coffin and with due respect, it was covered with a white sheet and flowers. Saji did keep recording a lot of the proceedings on his cellphone, probably to use it somewhere later, but one really can't grudge him that. His team shifted the coffin into the hearse and then led the way to the designated cemetery in his car. While I finished the formalities with the hearse driver, they had already shifted inside. The priest was surprisingly young and one of the volunteers assisted him with the rituals too. Though all the prayers were in Malayalam, the intonations were very soothing. After the rituals were over, Saji's team again took over and right from lowering the coffin into the grave, and the last prayers up to the ritual lighting of candles, they led all the way. He even promised to help in the laying of the tombstone a few days later as the team was too busy.

The Covid pandemic brought out the worst and also the best in our people. On the one hand, people were selling oxygen and drugs at a premium, in the black market and on the other, we had people like Saji (and his silent, efficient, and nameless volunteers) who went out of the way to help souls in distress. People who were absolute strangers came forward selflessly, to help a bereaved family in dire need of support and guidance. The way they did everything, right from arranging the coffin to being the pallbearers, was unbelievable. Even more so because it wasn't the first time for them or the last. And no money or compensation was expected or asked for. None at all!

Saji Varghese; India needs more people like you!

PS: JP came back to Surat a year later and we made a trip to the cemetery to pay our respects. There was a proper, formal tombstone in place. I wasn't aware when it had been done. Saji had taken care of it later, as promised.

Saji Varghese; India really needs more people like you

CHAPTER FOUR

THE SPICE OF LIFE

I have spent my entire life dodging what Indians are really fond of: spicy food.

To top it, I married into a family which is ardent about “masaledar’ food and have always been surrounded by friends who really adore the spicy stuff. By a quirk of fate or an anti-national gene, I seem to have no affinity for the ‘hot’ stuff. Not for me, the taste-bud-destroying red chilli powder or the hemorrhoid-inducing green chillies! No Sir! While this may be considered a dereliction of a national duty, I do have a primary responsibility for the well-being of both ends of my gastrointestinal tract!

For a person whose taste buds routinely go numb for two days after having a bite of something as innocent as capsicum, growing up in India posed an invisible challenge. I belong to that breed of humans who rejoice in the heavenly blandness of oats and thank God for creating the incredibly tasteless dragon fruit. The daal in the ‘Daal Tadka’ and the paneer in the “Paneer Butter Masala’ exist because of us! Left to the rest, restaurants would be serving only ‘Tadka’ and ‘Butter Masala’.

Two decades ago, there was a time when I actually had bhel and pani puri from roadside vendors. Nowadays the first thought on seeing a roadside pani puri or bhel vendor is that of Hepatitis A, stomach cramps and diarrhoea. The digestive tract was somewhat more resilient then. But still, while my gang was going "Bhaiya aur teekha banao!" I would be trying to gulp down his sweetest bhel mixtures with difficulty.

Street food was worse in another way; it was prepared right in front of you. Just looking at all the chopped chillies and the amount of spices being put in, can make the weak-hearted panicky! Be it bhel or pav bhaji, you can't really enjoy your food if looking at it reminds you of haemorrhoids!

Eating out in restaurants was always a challenge. Everyone wanted the masala something or the chilli something else, while you would break into a sweat thinking about not only the eating part but also the ordeal in store for the next morning. Half the meal time was spent digging out the green and red chilli peppers from the food with the diligence of an Archaeologist at Harappa. The world at large can never understand the technical difficulty of searching for green chillies in palak paneer or red ones in tomato-based gravies.

Looking at your extreme concentration, the waiters would become concerned that you had found dead insects in the food. This annoyed them because they had already removed all the live and moving ones from the food just before serving it to you! The Manager would start hovering around in case you decided to create a ruckus. Then you could almost hear his sigh of relief when he realised that you were one of those unpatriotic oddballs! Invariably, a few chillies were missed and all it took was one single, stupid bite of a milligram of the stuff to spoil the rest of the meal. The remaining time was spent mostly guzzling water, trying to douse the fires in one's mouth. Later, the

Manager fellow would also give you dirty looks when you stuffed your face with the mouth freshener to complete the fire fighting which nine litres of water had not been able to complete.

The hostel mess in the government medical college, where I studied was a partial blessing in disguise. In general, the food was quite unidentifiable. The daal looked and tasted like the muddy water from the community swimming pool, but was probably less hygienic. However, the food wasn't always bad. Once we even complimented the mess manager that the aloo gobi was very tasty, but the cook took offence because the dish was actually fruit custard. Sometimes there were dishes consisting of a lake of oil from which one had to ladle out stuff which looked and tasted like a mix of rotting seaweed and boiled leather. But those were special dishes, reserved for holidays and some festivals when there was a 'feast'. There was a rumour that the Medicine Dept borrowed this stuff to induce vomiting in their poisoning patients! On most other days it would have been impossible to find any taste even if the Pathology Dept tried searching for it with a microscope. But those blissful years were spent comparatively happily. No taste meant no spices which meant no heartburn.

Being born a Punjabi only added to the woes. In Punjabi cuisine, most dishes start with a bucket full of oil or ghee, to which is added a sackful of spices and chillies which are then allowed to interbreed. Then come the valiant tomatoes and onions, which Nature has created for the sole purpose of being massacred to make gravy for Punjabi food. This potent gas-forming mix is then poured into the nearest vessel and some vegetables are tossed in as an afterthought. That's the reason why the dishes have names like Veg Handi, Kadhai Paneer and Balti Chicken, the emphasis being more on the vessel and less on the food. The end product is generally a recipe for ulcers and haemorrhoids if you are lucky enough to survive the heart attack first. The poor vegetable or chicken or paneer, after which the dish is primarily named, hides scared in the depths, waiting for the loving, warm comfort of someone's gastric acids!

So much for trying to spice up life; I would rather bland it down!

CHAPTER FIVE

INDIANS ON A TRAIN

Some time ago, I had to travel to Mumbai to catch an overseas flight. I was grumbling about the fact that there were no international flights from my city, which is a hub of the textile and diamond industries. But on reaching the railway station I realised that I was travelling by rail after a long time. Nowadays, it is mostly a flight from Surat to somewhere and then a connection from there to somewhere else. But even after so many years, the railway station was as dirty, crowded and chaotic as I remembered.

The trip was by the recently introduced Vande Bharat Express and there was a whole crowd of people ready with their cellphones, jostling to record its majestic entry into the station. Stepping into the Executive Class coach almost made one forget that one was not abroad already. But the 'foreign wali' feeling went away immediately as the train was still full of my countrymen.

Three generations of a loud and emotive family were playing something like musical chairs but without the music. Then someone discovered that the seats could be rotated to face each other. This set off an intense contest of revolving chairs. Thankfully the meals hadn't been served otherwise, these revolutionaries (or is it revolvers?) would have been vomiting semi-digested rice and paneer all over the place.

The fooling around with the seats stopped once the food trays were served and all three generations settled down for dinner, setting off a new chain of problems. The juniors did not want to eat something or the other because it was yucky or because they were hungry only for something else, like a pizza. The seniors could not eat this or that because it gave them 'gas' or 'constipation'. One Uncle would then begin to describe in excruciating detail about his digestive troubles and how, with half the force he had to exert in the mornings, we could easily expel all illegal migrants from India. When he was about to elaborate upon the consistency, colour and texture, the embarrassed Aunty would hurriedly cut him off mid-sentence lest someone start vomiting.

The middle generation (which I can completely relate with) got down to juggling the nauseating and constipating food between the plates, thus achieving a semblance of order. In the process, they ended up with all the unwanted stuff on their plates and then sat down to have that with little joy, but immense relief. Anyway, all the food trays being passed around also ignited the hunger pangs in the other passengers who hadn't ordered train food.

Nowadays, the average Indian family, irrespective of ethnicity, can be seen at malls and fast food joints biting into fries or the glorified vada-pav called a burger or tucking into pizzas with enough cheese to finance a Cardiologist's family vacation to Europe with first-class airfare. But when travelling by rail, one could almost stereotype or profile people by the food they carry.

While roti and sabji are quite common, if there are bhujia and sweets in addition, then the origins of the passengers are from Rajasthan. My short stint in Tamil

Nadu revealed that Tamilians like to carry assorted types of rice and biryanis. People hailing from Uttar Pradesh prefer poori over rotis, with their sabji. Thepla and pickle are as distinctive of Gujarats as Donald Trump's hairdo or Amitabh Bachchcan's baritone. And if a family is having parathas oozing ghee along with at least 2 sabjis one of which looks like bits of paneer doing the backstroke in an oily onion and tomato gravy, then they are Punjabis without a doubt.

Also, it's a myth that food makes you sleepy. Because, after dinner, everyone around us seemed to be all charged up. The motions, gesturing, the volume of discussion and of the laughter all went up like petrol prices. Add to this the loud songs on cell phones, the raucous garba remixes, and the general drivel of Whatsapp videos, and the rail carriage seemed more like a Goa beach party. Fortunately for the rest, the last stop was near and the heart was filled with hope that there would soon be some peace. But alas, it wasn't to be.

Another typical Indian trait is the hurry to get on or off any form of transport. Maybe it has been coded into our genes after decades of jostling to get into and out of BEST buses, Mumbai local trains, state transport buses or the Delhi Metro. The trait resurfaces as soon as a bus or train halts or a boarding gate opens. What starts off as a single line, mostly ends up in a free-for-all all with no order or courtesy. I sometimes feel that drought victims display more poise when crowding for food packets than my country folk trying to board buses and trains. While the food packets may fall short, the flight is definitely not leaving without you.

This trait is on display in reverse also. Before a train stops, there is a long queue at the gate, which has been strategically blocked by someone with their luggage an hour in advance. While in a train, this is partly understandable, as there is generally a crowd of similarly genetically coded citizens waiting outside to push their way in. But the flight is not going anywhere till you get off folks! The rush to stand up as soon as the wheels touch the ground and the hurry to open the overhead storage and pull out the bags in each and every flight is laughable. The frustration of the poor flight attendants trying to control us is understandable.

There aren't any of those in trains and as soon as the train stops, there is always a mad melee to board and alight simultaneously and invariably, there will be this one passenger who will decide to use the toilets exactly at this time. He will fight valiantly against the incoming rush of people and suitcases and hold them up further. By the time he has done his business and is back with a smug look, the new entrants would generally have settled down and all is forgiven and forgotten.

Toilets in Indian trains are only slightly more appealing than Dhinchak Pooja's songs and probably less crappy. While the newer trains have closed systems and vacuum flushes, unfortunately, the people using the facilities remain the same. We have only devised more innovative methods to make a mess and leave them dirtier. The origins of this behaviour remain as a topic of research for a PhD seeker's thesis and we shall not tread there today.

Once we reached our station and managed to get off the train coach after being pushed back in twice, everyone was in a rush to reach their final destinations. There was another rush to reach the autorickshaw stand, the taxi stand or the Uber pick-up point.

We Indians are a unique species, always in a hurry but almost never on time!

CHAPTER SIX

MORE INDIANS ON ANOTHER TRAIN

On another rail trip, the lady sitting next to me got a call from her daughter even before the train pulled out from our boarding station. She was returning from a wedding. She had been treated well by one relative and not so well by another, and was dissatisfied, as it is customary to be, at Indian weddings. She and her daughter compared the amounts in their 'return gift' envelopes. She checked and discovered that she had got Rs 250 while the daughter had got 150. According to the unwritten and poorly understood laws governing the 'give and take' during weddings, this was unacceptable. A few more calls confirmed that the 250 was the wrong amount for the relatives on this side. After a Forensic inspection of the envelope, Mrs Holmes deduced that she had been given someone else's envelope. After another round of phone calls, it was confirmed that there was another lady with the same name on the hosts' in-laws' side and thus the mix-up.

After this, I was privy to the intimate family politics of the Shah and the Jain families and how this mix-up of a hundred rupees would affect the generations to come. Apparently, there could be a family feud lasting for centuries like what happened in Bollywood movies, or some ancestors would rise from the dead and then die again, or maybe the DNA of subsequent generations of the 'other side' would be corrupted and their offsprings would be born with 'Mera baap kanjoos hai' tattooed on their forearms.

Apart from loudly discussing family and business matters on the phone, we are also fond of watching YouTube and WhatsApp videos at full volume, without earphones. The viewer always feels that the YouTube videos, Insta reels and Facebook posts are absolutely hilarious or informative. also, it is their phone, and the sound emanating from that also belongs to them. Not only do you have no right to object to the high volume, on the contrary, you are trespassing on their sound without their consent!

A decade or more ago the phones were less smart but the people were largely still idiots. In those days, there always used to be an Uncleji in one of the cabins, who would be dispensing 'desi' knowledge to his fellow passengers about how to treat constipation by breathing through one nostril and dripping some exotic oil in the other one; or saying goodbye to blood pressure by meditating with cows. Later he would be describing how to fight Dengue with papaya seeds, or the benefits of drinking honey mixed with cow dung, or the anti-depressant properties of neem. There was always an anecdote about a distant relative who had 'full' diabetes and drank some Babaji's magic mix of karela (a hot favourite in all desi recipes), lauki, tinda and green chillies dissolved in gaumutra, at exactly 4:46 AM following a full moon night, and never had to take another medicine again in his lifetime.

From dental caries to divorce, Uncleji had a solution for everything. The salient features of any such solutions were:

1. It was 'desi' and hence there were no side effects.
2. It did not necessitate going to a doctor (because doctors are worse than the disease itself)
3. It was pure veg!
4. It was free, free, free.

A simple way to avoid Uncleji was to walk down to the open space near the doors where the smell emanating from the toilets was less nauseating than the recipes being discussed. Rarely, one could find a vacant place in another cabin till Uncleji ran out of steam.

Nowadays life is no longer so simple. Now, if you shift to another cabin, the recipe playing on your neighbour's phone just changes from Murgh Musallam to Maa ki Daal or from Chocolate Maggi to Fanta omelette, each more disgusting than the other. Uncleji's rants of morality and nauseating remedies actually begin to seem appealing in comparison to the whooping laugh and the annoying "Oh no no no no no" of TikTok videos, the senseless Insta reels and the pointless YouTube Shorts. Or the loud 'hello' 'hello' of the passenger beside you, on a bad network where the person on the phone sincerely feels that shouting louder will make the signals better. Or the bratty kids who start bawling if the parent's mobile is taken away from them for even one second! How I miss the good old days!

Then there were the rounds of the TTE (Traveling Ticket Examiner) every time the duty changed. This was the pre-internet era when one actually had to carry a ticket issued by Indian Railways and an ID proof. The TTE was the Lord of the Berths and would be immediately surrounded near the vestibule, by a crowd of waitlisted passengers each hankering for a 'confirmed' berth. It always started with "seat nahi hai", then some cash would silently change hands and magically the seats would appear and the crowd would dissolve, everyone happily going to settle down in their allotted berths. Nowadays, I travel only short distances by train, that too mostly in the AC Chair Car coaches. The TTEs rarely ask for any ID proofs, are much better dressed and definitely much more polite. The toilets, on the other hand, are just as dirty and smelly!

CHAPTER SEVEN

THE ANGST OF A FAT GUY

George Orwell once said that there is a thin man inside every fat man. I relate more with Homer who felt that he was an obese man trapped in a fat man's body.

One has to admit that, the rounder the infants or kids, the more adorable they are. The little ones with the extra baby fat are the ones whose waddle is also more 'awww' inducing. And who doesn't like pulling the cheeks of a cute, chubby cherub? These are also the ones to whom you will probably give that extra cookie or toffee. And add to their future woes...

Being an obese or overweight child entails carrying around so much more than just the extra kilos. Every fat kid has been teased about his or her weight at some time. No matter how active or agile they are, the obese kids are often the butt of jokes. Yet, being called fatso, motu, jaadiya or gundu is often taken in good humour. Who wants to be a spoilsport? But it does hurt. Somewhere inside, deep within, beyond the cellulite, it hurts!

Growing up is hard; growing up fat even more so. Teenage brings its own set of problems. By now, one is somewhat used to the constant reminders of the tyres spilling over the beltline. While the hipster crowd is into the latest trends, the heavyweights try to hide under loose, baggy clothing. But it really doesn't help. At the beginning and end of the day, you do see yourself in the mirror. Poor self-image leads to a very difficult interaction with the opposite sex. The fear of ridicule and rejection is stronger in this sub-species than in the regular, garden variety, gawky teenager. That's why you often see the whales paired together in colleges. Probably, they find solace in each other. And they can enjoy that samosa and jalebi, away from the judgemental gaze of some skinny freak.

Society does accept them in its own way.

Fun fact: in eastern and north-eastern India, people who are well-built, stocky or plain fat, are called "Punjabi' body. Whereas in Punjab, the fat ones are accepted as the norm. In fact, here the euphemism for obese is 'healthy'. So, 'a little healthy' means overweight, 'quite healthy' means clinically obese by a dozen kilos and 'very healthy' means that your Cardiologist starts planning a Europe tour every time you book an appointment. So. if your Punjabi friend's mother refers to you as 'healthy' don't be euphoric. She is calling you fat in her own kind way.

Have you noticed, that adult obese men are among the jolliest people you come across? Is it nature's gift or is it just an attempt to disguise a more deep-seated insecurity? The fat ones can often be found eyeing the thin ones with silent (but not malevolent) envy, especially at meal times. It is quite distressing to see all the calories from pizzas and ice creams magically evaporating from your thin friends' skins while even your stupid, unsweetened, organic, green tea makes you gain weight!

And it's not that we have not tried to lose weight. There is no diet and no exercise regimen which has been left out.

Keto diet, Atkins, Mediterranean, Subterranean, Martian; Caveman, Batman, Superman: we've tried them all! Pilates, Yoga, weights, cardio, Zumba: been there, done that! Nothing works! No matter how active they are, the image of the fat guy is mostly that of a lazy and lethargic person. And the amount of unsolicited advice you get to exercise or workout or eat "healthy' is unbelievable. Oh hello! There is something called genetics too. Mind your own business folks!

Every overweight person's wardrobe has a special section; clothes which are two sizes too small, bought years ago with a definite plan to fit into them in two months' time. A plan so strong that it broke a wall made of Ambuja cement, so precise that three Swiss watches developed an inferiority complex on meeting it. But when the Incredible Hulk of a plan met the Incredible Bulk of a man, the plan retreated respectfully and hid out of sight, waiting to be recalled another day.

A small step for a plan, a giant step for plankind!

Buying clothes is another major pain. From an obese person's perspective, any garment shop or outlet has only three sections: XXL, 'this will never fit" and "Why did I even come here?". Forget about fashion, finding and fitting into basic clothes is a nightmare. And who are the idiots who make XXL and XXXL size clothes in "slim fit"? I mean, what's the idea of sending an already troubled person on another guilt trip? And buying clothes online? Just forget about it! Trying to find your size specifications on a website is more difficult than teaching Shakespeare to a drunken monkey!

Fatsos of the world, it is time to unite! Raise your voices now or forever hold your silence. It is the time to rise in revolt against this heartless world! Obesity is officially an epidemic and very soon there will be more of us fat guys than these evil, thin ones!

Low-fat yoghurt, fat-free ice cream and air fryers should be declared illegal. Fat-free ice cream was always a scam. Ice cream without fat is only ice! And my opinion of air-fried food is best left unsaid!

All the stocks of the world's protein shakes, green tea, green coffee beans and garcinia should be set alight in public and their sale outlawed for eternity.

Never again should an obese fellow be subjected to the tyranny of weight loss supplements!

But all said and done we are remarkably thick-skinned. We mostly don't care two hoots for what others think. Move along people. We are happy enough as we are.

Even the scriptures say that he who obese the commands of God, will one day rule the girth!

CHAPTER EIGHT

IN THE MIDDLE OF LIFE

On a road trip to Mumbai, we were stuck in the mother, father and a younger sister of all traffic jams, at three different places. If someone else is driving, a traffic jam is a good time to reflect upon life. Given the total standstill, I mainly wondered about two things: how any work gets done at all in Mumbai, because Mumbaikars seem to reside in their cars and in the BEST buses and local trains; and why Mumbai does not produce more philosophers of the stature of Plato, Sartre or the 'Made in India' Devdas. At some point of time when the only thing moving was a random train of thought, a sudden realization dawned! This situation was similar to a mid-life crisis.

Mid-life sneaks up on you suddenly when one day a densely bearded, twenty-something calls you "Uncle'. Only then do you realize that the trousers are too tight, the belt holes have shifted by a few inches and the hairline has receded, just like all sense has from today's TV debates! Coming to terms with the new status quo, you move on, till on another not-so-fine day you have the feeling that life is in a rut, not going anywhere.

Welcome to the mid-life crisis: the traffic jam of life!

Life, which was cruising smoothly like a Ferrari, now seems to behave like an overheated Ambassador with a blocked carburettor. In general, life seems to be going nowhere. Everyone else seems to be making progress while you are stuck in the same place. The fellow next to you somehow seems to find a way and moves ahead. You know he will again get stuck, maybe a little ahead of you. But the problem is that he found a way and you did not. Once in a while, some jerk cuts in between the traffic and magically finds a way out of the mess. And you again feel like a loser for not having the guts to do that!

Everyone seems to be having more fun than you do. If you look at FB or Insta, every bloody bugger is enjoying life while you are wondering why you became a doctor or engineer or lawyer in the first place. Even the vacations you go on seem to lack the fun and frolic of the Insta and FB crowd. It's the same feeling you get when looking out of your car window and seeing the group in the car beside you laughing and joking as if they are on a picnic, while even your car AC seems to be having a mid-life crisis of its own.

Traffic jams have three stages: denial, realization and 'to hell with it'! So does a mid-life crisis.

When in the jam, initially you are hopeful that soon you will be back on track. Similarly in life, you hope that all the troubles go away and you go back to whatever slightly happier phase you were in. Then you begin to suspect that life has a different plan for you. The only problem is that life, sadistically, refuses to tell you what the bloody plan is!

Once you step out of denial, you realize that nothing seems to be going right. Every turn taken till now seems to have been the wrong one. The ifs and the butts, both keep getting bigger! We would have been better off if we had left earlier or taken that road instead of this one or come by train or not stopped for lunch.... Or, I shouldn't have become a doctor, I should have become a stock trader, I could have been the next Jhunjhunwala, I should have done engineering and become a stand-up comic later. Or at least, I could become a model for all the 'before' photos for weight loss products. All decisions taken previously seem to have gone wrong; including those which you were not responsible for, like being born.

As many great men (Mahatma Gandhi, Steve Jobs, Albert Einstein, Chanakya to name a few) have often said on WhatsApp, 'This too shall pass'. And it does. The traffic clears slowly and you get moving again and finally reach wherever you had set out to go. So too in life, you finally do move on. This holds true for most people.

Most, not all!

And this is where the third stage kicks in. Some drivers suddenly decide that enough is enough and do something rash like cut across lanes, try to move out into a side lane and find a magical new path to their destination; to boldly go where no man has gone before. Similarly, the soul with the receding hairline and the protruding belly, too makes some crazy decisions which seem completely rational to him. The flashy cars, which look like a deranged teenager's fantasy, the age-inappropriate behaviour, and the extramarital affairs; are all just different methods of trying to break free from the traffic jam of mid-life. And like on the road, they generally never turn out well. After the initial thrill or gratification, one realizes that cutting across the traffic actually did not work and only achieved a show of middle fingers and a barrage of abuses.

Time is the greatest teacher and the biggest healer.

To conclude, I quote my friend Vikram J, (he used to say this often when we were in Medical College, but it has taken me more than 2 decades to understand his wise words):

"In the middle of life, there is always an if!"

CHAPTER NINE

I'LL BE BACK IN JUST A MINUTE

A patient who had consulted me wanted to know if he could take a drug called "Horny Goat Weed Extract" along with his other medications. I had never heard of this stuff before, and I confessed the same to him. Later, I brewed a cup of coffee and sat down to Google this exotic aphrodisiac (strictly for professional reasons!). Just as I was about to learn the secret magical powers of this wonder drug, there was a notification on a WhatsApp group.

An idiot I did not like, had posted some stupid, unfunny thing on a group which I had joined against my wish. I left my research for a minute to post a fitting reply to the egoistic, self-centred moron. I had managed to compose a savage reply when there was this message on one of the Finance groups. I would just come back in a minute to show this fellow his place.

There was a hot tip on the Stocks group. Scamsindia Ltd was touted to be the next big multi-bagger. The person who gave this tip had given a similar tip a few months ago and I had bought a truckload of shares. Unfortunately, the promoter's dog, who was also his accountant, had fallen ill and died. Since the company accounts had all been maintained in a mix of barks, howls and paw prints, no one could decipher anything and so everyone's money was stuck. The poor, bereaved promoter was so sad that he left the country and settled in London.

But such mishaps don't happen every day. Today's tip looked like a great company with excellent prospects. Their balance sheet was full of numbers and ratios which I did not understand, which proved that they were genuine. The promoters had been jailed for financial fraud only twice and their head office was located somewhere in Jamtara, with a branch in Nigeria; how inspiring! I didn't have much money left over after that poor dog died, but I decided to borrow some and invest; the opportunity was too good to miss. Just then, there was this notification on Facebook. I would come back and do my investing in just a minute.

My neighbour, who I had just met in the morning today, had just posted his vacation pics from Maldives. Apparently, he had been in Maldives for the last month, enjoying his liver to death. And stupid me! I had met him in the elevator just this morning and the crafty fellow had totally convinced me that he was actually standing there with me when he was actually snorkelling somewhere in the Indian Ocean. Anyway, let him enjoy. I 'liked' his pics, and posted a cheesy 'awwww'. I planned to tell him to keep enjoying himself in Maldives when I met him again in the evening today.

I scrolled down and there was this genius demonstrating the correct way to cook Fanta Maggi. I thought of tracing him to murder him, but just then there was another MasterChef showing his recipe for Chocolate pav-bhaji. Oh, the horror! But thankfully, he then said that you could make it very healthy by using dark chocolate, instead of regular milk chocolate; which was an immense relief. Can you imagine how unhealthy regular chocolate would have been?

I scrolled down further to an FB live session. A very sincere gentleman was trying to sell some very effective hair growth oils for just Rs 99,000/- only! He appeared to be an introvert because he wouldn't show his face and his email and phone numbers were also all hidden away. He just requested his clients to send him the money in advance and he would ship the product. I had been troubled by my receding hairline for many months now. Since this introverted fellow also appeared quite needy (that's why he wanted the payment in advance, isn't it?), I was just deciding which money to send to him: the kids' school fees or the home loan EMI, when the Telegram app notified me of a new message. I would just come back in a minute to help this poor chap.

There was this Telegram channel where people shared books. There were magazines, textbooks, novels and whatnot. Someone had shared some new magazines in Swahili and a very serious-looking textbook. I downloaded the magazines; they would be useful if I happened to learn Swahili someday. I also downloaded the Textbook of Animal Psychiatry, just in case I needed it someday. I had more than 7000 such wonderful books on my hard drive, which I plan to read someday. I think I may need a new hard disk soon though. The Insta app pinged and I decided to come back in a minute to sort out the space on my hard drive.

A person who I followed on Insta had posted a reel which was a YouTube short of a TikTok video which had been copied from FB and converted into an Insta reel. The person had converted the post so many times that he was no longer sure of which religion he followed now!

Haha!

Hilarious, isn't it?

No?

You fellows can't appreciate intellectual humour. You wouldn't know the difference between a fool posting an Insta reel and an idiot posting a TikTok video.

Because there is no difference!

Haha!

Got you again. I told you I'm hilarious!

Anyway, there wasn't any more time for my rib-tickling humour because YouTube had sent a notification that my favourite stand-up comic had posted a new video. I would come back to Telegram in a minute after checking the new video. The video was actually somewhat longer than a minute and after about 5 minutes, I realized that this video wasn't funny at all. But once I start something, I don't get distracted easily and don't rest till the job is done. So I spent the next 45 minutes watching the whole video which was actually quite boring. A total waste of time, it had been. So I decided to watch another video to lighten my mood and started surfing YouTube to look for something watchable. About 20 minutes later, I was still undecided whether to watch a conspiracy theory about aliens spreading Covid or the unadulterated bovine excreta from a famous motivational speaker. I would have wasted my whole day in indecision, but Twitter (now 'X') saved me.

I just saw that a very annoying fellow, who I followed, had posted something equating not paying taxes with being unpatriotic. How dare he speak sense? Though I agreed with the general tenor of his post, my dislike for him made me post a sharp retort about him going to Pakistan if he didn't like the way things worked in India. Suits him right! Being so annoying and yet speaking sense? How could anyone tolerate such bigotry? But why was I wasting my time on this chap when I had so many better things to do?

This reminded me that I had been reading up about some new drug, something important, something to do with howling goats or was it roasted oats? Anyway, I'll come to that in a minute; there is an interesting thread I need to check on Reddit.

It won't take long. I'll be back in just a minute!

CHAPTER TEN

THE COBBLER UNDER THE TREE

I joined Medical College in 1992. Near our campus was a Fire Station. Just outside stood a tree under which sat a cobbler with his box full of tools and stuff. He was actually quite good at his craft and we used his services often. Nobody knew his name. It was always "Bhaiya' do this and 'Bhaiya' do that. He was a nameless worker who toiled away, eking out a living.

The years passed and I progressed in life and in my career. After MBBS, I did a Master's in General Surgery and then further speciality training in Urology. All these years I must have passed the Fire Station and the tree a thousand times and seen the cobbler at work. While I had climbed the ladder of success, he still sat in the same place after almost two decades, doing the same drudgery. But in the race of life, the mission was to keep running lest one falls behind, and the cobbler was just another nameless face, often seen, sometimes used and easily forgotten.

After I returned to my city in 2008 as a qualified Urologist, I used to offer Honorary service at the Municipal Medical College for many years. The patient load was tremendous and the waiting list for surgeries was very long.

Frequently, people would come for a consultation at my private chambers and then try to leverage that to get a priority appointment for surgeries at the College. Some would even offer to pay money 'under the table' to jump the queue. This never materialized for anyone and was a frequent cause of discontent.

One day, the cobbler walked into my OPD. I recognised him at once, and for the first time in more than 20 years, I became aware that his name was Sudama. Apparently, his brother was posted for prostate surgery on my next list at the college. I could make out that they had come just to see if they needed to complete any 'formalities' so that the surgery went through on schedule. In simpler terms, they wanted to know if they needed to pay me anything. After reassuring them that nothing was required, I sent them off and the surgery was done on schedule after a few days.

Thereafter, every time I crossed the Fire Station, the cobbler had a name and an identity. I no longer disregarded his presence. Now, he too would wave back in acknowledgement if he noticed my car passing by. Suddenly he became human!

Now that he was a human, I started wondering how tough it would have been for him to make ends meet with the menial work he had been doing for so long. For as long as I could remember, he had sat and worked under that tree. In contrast, I reflected upon my own progress in life.

When I was a medical student, Sudama sat there.

When I became a General Surgeon, he was in the same spot.

Today, I have been practising as a Urologist for more than 15 years and he is still there.

When we used to walk to every place, because we had no personal vehicles, Sudama used to sit there and repair shoes and chappals.

When we rode our bikes, he was there.

When I drove my first car, the Maruti 800, he was there.

Today, I drive around in an SUV and Sudama still sits there.

When I stayed in a dilapidated government hostel and shared my room with two others, he sat and worked there.

Today, I stay in a spacious apartment and run my own hospital and Sudama is still repairing people's damaged footwear.

The cobbler under the tree getting a name somehow gave a new perspective to life. Actually, there is nothing new, it is just something most of us choose not to think or talk about; about what we have, rather than what we don't!

When was the last time that you met someone who was content and satisfied with what they had in life?

How many people do you know of, who think they earn enough?

How many people can you recall, who never complain about how much they work / comparatively how little they earn / how difficult life is / how they are struggling in life? Finding it tough to think of even two names, isn't it? That is the unfortunate truth.

It has almost become fashionable to rant about one's struggles and problems in life. In the race to become bigger and better and wealthier, rarely do we reflect upon how much we have already achieved and how good life has been till now. Look around and you will see a Sudama everywhere, someone who is toiling away day and night and barely making ends meet. See him and at least sometimes give a thought to how far you have come in life.

We are living the life which is someone's dream.

We stay in houses which most people cannot think of owning after a lifetime of labour.

Our children go to schools which our own parents were never able to afford for us.

We earn in a day what a million others can't earn in months.

And yet it is we who say that life is difficult!

CHAPTER ELEVEN

THE HINDI HEARTLAND DETOUR

The year was 2001 and I had gone to appear for the super-specialty entrance exam at Sanjay Gandhi Post Graduate Institute (SGPGI), Lucknow, after getting my Master of Surgery degree. After the exam at SGPGI was over, I still had 2 days left. This was my first attempt at the exam and I had over-optimistically booked my return ticket for 3 days later, assuming that I would do well, and would have to appear for the viva. I was a gold medallist in General Surgery after all. And so, I hadn't formally prepared for the exam either. Alas! The SGPGI entrance was a totally different level of difficulty. There were about 200 questions, of which I could understand about 20. How many of those were answered correctly is completely irrelevant.

Now I had another couple of days to nurse my bruised and battered ego and nothing to do in Lucknow. So I called my friend RS and planned a trip to his town, Shahjahanpur the next day. He promised to come to pick me up from the station. Just in case he could not come, I was to take an auto to Chamkani Fatakiya and he stayed just nearby. A full-fledged railway crossing is a 'faatak' and this was a small crossing, so a 'fatakiya'. Armed with this knowledge, I set off to meet my old friend on his home ground.

He worked as a Medical Officer at some peripheral Primary Health Center and I was worried how he would get leave to come and meet me. I need not have worried. He used to visit his workplace occasionally, mostly when some senior was visiting. The rest of the time, he was at home studying for entrance exams. Not a very flattering picture of the health infrastructure in Uttar Pradesh (UP), but India worked that way then and still does in many places. Anyway, improving UP's healthcare was not on my agenda and I set off for Shahjahanpur looking forward to meeting an old friend.

On reaching there, the great RS was nowhere to be found. I called him up and he assured me that he was on the way. I cursed him for the sixteen rupees spent on the outgoing call from my mobile. In those days, incoming calls were also charged some 5 to 8 rupees per minute, a far cry from the almost unlimited talk time and data available today on most cellular services. After about half an hour, bhai showed up, on a motorcycle, on the passenger seat. Having stayed in a hostel for years, I was no stranger to triple-seat riding, but with my luggage, this was really stretching the limit. But he had specially borrowed the vehicle (and its owner too, apparently) to pick me up. Refusing to use this vehicle could be considered an act of war, so I ended up riding triple seat, on a motorcycle, with a biggish bag hanging on one side and a suitcase on the other. Praying hard and holding tight onto my luggage and hoping that I wouldn't fall off at one of the million potholes, we finally reached his house.

We caught up over chai and pakoras and in the evening we took a stroll through the local market. Suddenly we were crossed by three people on bicycles. Innocuous enough, if it hadn't been for the double barrel rifles slung on their shoulders! People moving around with guns in a crowded marketplace was a new experience and being a true Indian at heart, I stared at them!

Much later, after endless chatting, when we turned in for the night, I was told about the toilet situation. In case I hadn't noticed already, there was no running water and I would have to use a bucket if required. Of course, there was a light bulb there but sometimes there were power cuts, so a torch was also provided for any emergency. I was a special guest and was very well looked after.

The trip ended much too quickly and the next morning, I was dropped off at the railway station. Thankfully, this time we were on two bikes and there was no triple-seat riding. I took a slow train back to Lucknow, from Shahjahanpur. The journey would take about 6 hours or so. True to form, RS stayed with me till the train left the station.

To my pleasant surprise, on the train, I could get a seat very easily in the unreserved coach and I settled down with my novel. There was a young lady with her small kid, one Uncleji type and a couple of other insignificant characters seated in the space for six. The kid migrated to the window and the men indulged in irrelevant small talk. The lady too joined in at some point in time, which was a bit of a surprise to me. After some time, she apparently countered the Uncleji type, whose 'UP male' ego got hurt quickly. The argument grew heated, and Uncleji lost whatever was left of his cool. The atmosphere became very tense and the insignificant characters shrunk away, while I tried to remain engrossed in my book. I was a bit worried for the lady as, after all, this was the notorious, patriarchal, misogynist heartland of Uttar Pradesh.

I needn't have worried. The woman stood her ground and gave as good as she got. When he couldn't counter her logically, Uncleji got flustered and shouted "Maryada nahi hai tum mein!" (loosely translated as: you don't know your limit, woman!) and then had to be pacified by the insignificant characters while the lady glared away without fear or remorse. He had met his match in a woman half his age and had to back off reluctantly.

This episode broke the stereotype, in my mind, of the weak, voiceless and submissive UP female. On the contrary, she was a fighter, not cowed down by the predatory or aggressive male and ready to stand her ground. She was not the frightened and submissive being that I had imagined. UP's future wasn't so bleak after all.

PS: RS went on to become a renowned super-specialist consultant and settled in a city near his home town, where he is a very reputed and respected personality. More than two decades after my trip, RS's wife contested the local elections and became a Member of the Legislative Assembly in UP. I hear that she also has a solid reputation locally for her good work in her constituency.

CHAPTER TWELVE

GYM DIARIES: THE BEGINNING

After a lot of vacillating and some serious effort on the part of my wife, I finally joined a gym. The gym manager was very accommodating. He explained all the packages and inclusions and then suggested that I go for the annual membership because it was the most economical. Now, I had read about this scam previously and knew that they always ask you to go for the annual package because they know that you will drop out and stop coming to the gym after a few days, at best a few weeks. But I wasn't going to be tricked so easily. I played some reverse psychology on him. Since he would be expecting me to avoid the annual subscription, and would try to convince me to go for that, to fool him, I took the annual membership without any resistance. The naive chap would never realise how he had been conned!

I was then given the option of getting a trainer to guide me. The trainers were categorised according to their place in the evolutionary ladder. The premium trainer resembled a gorilla on steroids and was supposed to have some human traits like being able to talk in complete sentences. The standard trainer looked similar but was not on steroids and could speak basic words like "Squat", "Down", "Up", " One more set", "Two more reps" and "Cardio". The basic level trainer looked a bit similar to the above types but would communicate only in grunts which you would have to decipher by yourself. Since I was going to come here to exercise, not to chat and gossip; and I did not have the time to learn primate languages; I opted for the standard trainer and decided to start from the next day.

After going home to a visibly happier spouse, I was asked to start preparing for the gym. I thought she meant that I should eat light that night and sleep well. Sadly, that wasn't the case. Apparently, going to the gym isn't as simple as getting up, wearing shoes and driving down in your night suit. Gym etiquette is a fine balance of sartorial, nutritional and physiological adjustment.

The first step was getting proper clothes. The clothes which I had planned to wear to the gym the next day (my usual night dress) were rejected outright. I protested that I had been wearing them every day without any problem for the last two years. But, as usual, I just did not understand. No self-respecting wife could let her husband go to a gym in such clothes. So I was taken to shop for clothes and other essential apparel. Mind you! I was taken, not sent! The first requirement for gymming is to be properly dressed in some branded clothes. So we bought some very expensive T-shirts and track pants made with some fancy material called driathlon or cottathlon or something similar which started absorbing your sweat even before you started sweating.

Buying gym socks is a science. Ideal gym socks are soft but firm, supportive but not compressive, short and long enough, keep the feet dry but don't become wet themselves, and absorb odours but don't become smelly......a study of the properties could make for a Ph.D.

thesis. I asked the shop assistant to give me two pairs of suitably expensive ones and let the matter rest there. At the gym, you also need a hand towel to wipe your sweat. I needed one right then looking at the exorbitant prices, and ended up buying two of those too.

I was now made to realise that one has to carry a proper water bottle too. The old Bisleri or Kinley bottle (with the label torn off) is not at all acceptable. Did I not have any concern for my image? I protested that the job of the bottle was to carry and provide water when I was thirsty, not build my image. The bloody bottle was so expensive, and on top of it, it was empty. My Bisleri bottle cost so much less and its price included the water inside too! But we men are like that; we just don't understand. Anyway, a bottle worthy of my social status was eventually purchased and we moved on to the shoe section.

I protested again that I had perfectly good shoes, purchased only eight years ago which were as good as new because I had rarely used them. With a smirk and rolled eyeballs, I was informed that what I had were walking shoes, and for the gym, I needed gym shoes which were different in a way that I would never understand so..... I quickly purchased what I was told to without further ado. Now that we were done with the clothes, we moved on to the nutritional supplements shop.

I was planning to hydrate myself with water but apparently, that is suicidal! One can choose from a million pre-, intra- and post-gym supplements to avoid the unpardonable sin of drinking plain water. Before the gym you should have caffeine and if looking for weight loss, green coffee bean extract. During the workout, you have to keep sipping BCAA (Branched Chain Amino Acid) solution. It is supposed to be very good for something important which no one seems to be very clear about. But everyone is clear about one thing; if you don't drink BCAA, then you will definitely die fat and be reborn as a one-eyed, mentally retarded monkey. I didn't think that hanging on trees would do any good for my social status, so I promptly bought one box.

And then, it was the turn of the holy grail: protein powder. There are more types of protein powders available in the market than there are proteins in nature. You can choose from casein, whey, whey isolate, single whey isolate, double purified isolate, with or without bioenzyme, with or without creatine, with or without glutamine or L-arginine, semi-digested, pre-digested, pre-eaten and regurgitated; you name it and it was available. Again, sensing that there was no escaping this expense, I asked the storekeeper to give me 250 gms of a simple whey protein brand. So he immediately gave me one kilogram of the most expensive, fully loaded powder because it was imported and 'A-one best quality'.

As he later told me, after using this protein powder, two of his customers, who had originally weighed a hundred and twenty kgs went on to win the Miss India contest, in spite of the fact that they were males; it was so good. Ekdum A-one, best quality, imported stuff, it was. Even though the label "Made in Honk Gong" appeared a little suspicious, I still bought it. After all, winning the Miss India title is no easy feat, mind you!

Now I was all set for my gym class and raring to attack the weights! That night I dreamed of the muscular, V-shaped body that I would be coming back with after my first day at the gym.

CHAPTER THIRTEEN

GYM DIARIES: CLOSE ENCOUNTER

The first morning, my wife readied my daughter for school and me for the gym. We were both provided with a bag, socks, shoes, towel, sipper bottles and I had a bonus cup of black coffee. The thin freaks of the world may not know that black coffee before a workout is good for fat loss. The only thing which my daughter had, but I did not, was a handkerchief tacked to the front of my T-shirt with a safety pin, with which I could wipe my nose!

Armed with all the paraphernalia, I set off on my quest to battle the bulge. The gym was on the 4th floor of a commercial complex. As I waited for the elevator, the first thing which struck me was that none of the fitness freaks used the stairs to go upstairs. I too was in the lift, which wasn't a morally very high ground, so I kept my peace. I had been instructed by my wife to change from my dirty slippers to gym shoes before entering and I did just that. After this, they made me enter my name and entry time in a register; which was another pointless tradition. The same ritual is followed in all apartment complexes in India. Many times, when visiting friends, I have entered my name as Hrithik Roshan, Baba Ramdev and sometimes Madhuri

Dixit, in the register kept at the reception, and nobody has ever bothered to read it. But here I signed my own name. I could have done otherwise, but Ratan Tata would have become really confused if he got a call from the gym to give them 5 stars on Google!

As I entered the gym a huge fellow who looked like Chacha Chaudhary's sidekick, Sabu, lumbered towards me. He looked at me for a few seconds, grunted "Cardio!" and pointed towards the treadmills. A cool dude was comfortably running at 15 kmph. I stopped and started staring at him in awe. I must have burned 100 calories just observing him running and yet staying in the same place. More than a century ago, in "Through The Looking Glass", Lewis Carroll had predicted this day when the Red Queen told Alice that "it takes all the running you can do, to keep in the same place. If you want to get somewhere else, you must run at least twice as fast as that"!

Anyway, I started at 5 kmph and expected Sabu to call me off shortly to do the real stuff, the weights and all. After three minutes, I was huffing and puffing and wheezing. There wasn't enough oxygen in the room. Something was wrong with the ACs also. And the treadmill was also defective; 5 kmph couldn't be so fast. The whole gym was grossly mismanaged. Sabu came to me and said "20 minutes". What? I needed at least 3 days to acclimatise myself to the low oxygen levels here. Mount Everest had more oxygen than this dump. And better weather too!

After the twenty minutes were over, I lay down beside the treadmill. "This is how it will finally end" I thought as my life started flashing before my eyes. I became sure that it was all over as it began to get darker. But it was only Sabu bending over me and blocking out the lights. I was expecting him to help me get up and respectfully escort me down to my car, but Sabu had other ideas. He just said "Legs!" and I remembered that mine were still attached to my torso. He showed me the machines for the leg press, calf raises, quadriceps extensions, hamstrings etc. But we would begin with squats. Gym trainers all over the Universe (even on those planets where the aliens don't have any legs) have a concept that squats are the best fat-burning exercise ever. So I did squats. After 2, my legs were wobbly; after 5, I was getting tremors all over, and after 10 I was at serious risk of toppling over, into the arms of Arnold (the God of all gyms) whose photos were all over the place. If you go to a gym anywhere in the world, I am sure there will be at least one photo of Arnold on its walls.

Sabu was a tough cookie; a tough, tasteless, sugar-free, fat-free and brain-free cookie. After my near tryst with Arnold, he made me do about 3000 more squats. By the end of 3 sets, my whole body was on fire. The gym manager had promised me that my fat would just melt away. Probably the fire was the way that it would happen. I started looking at the floor around me, but there was no puddle of melted fat anywhere. By now, I had no idea if my legs were still attached to my body or had fallen off.

I feigned giddiness and lay down on a bench. Sabu made me sit up and drink the BCAA solution which looked like Rooh Afza, smelled like urine and tasted like cough syrup. The brain woke up but the legs were still missing in action. I wobbled towards the exit, but Sabu blocked my way and said "Weights"! What? I had naively thought one near-death experience on the treadmill was enough for the day.

Before my man got any more ideas, I pointed to my wrist and said "Late! Emergency!" and shuffled towards the exit. By the time he registered that my phone had not rung and that I wasn't wearing a watch, I would be sufficiently far away from his reach. But he moved aside and actually spoke five words in a row. "Ok. Chest, shoulder, triceps tomorrow" after which he sat down to recover from the effort it took to do so.

I somehow reached my car, happy at just coming out alive and once inside, I looked down to confirm that my legs hadn't fallen off. I reached home expecting a hero's welcome. But instead, I was given a 'healthy' breakfast of a measured cup of milk and a sad-looking, malnourished paratha with severe butter deficiency.The rest of the day wasn't any better. Lunch was similar to breakfast in its calorie count and lack of appeal. Also, nobody commented even once on how fit I looked that day. All that exercise and not a single person noticed my new, improved version.

That night, I only dreamt of volcanoes erupting on Jupiter if I did something to make Sabu angry. The next morning, all my muscles were sore and protesting the punishment of the day before. I definitely needed a break.

It was good that I had paid for the whole year; I could go again for any number of days for one whole year.

But not today.

Maybe tomorrow!

CHAPTER FOURTEEN

THE SHOES OUTSIDE THE CHURCH

I spent a good part of my childhood in Bombay. It was still Bombay, in the 80s, when we were kids; it officially became Mumbai much later. We used to stay in Bandra West, a suburb full of Catholics. Every year, my class in school had a flock of D'Mellos, D'Souzas, Fernandez' and Perreiras. 'What man' and 'A man' were a must in any spoken sentence even though the teachers constantly reminded us that this was not how English was spoken. They were wrong! This was not how English was written in school. In Bandra West, this was exactly how English was spoken! Hindi was murdered at a totally different level but let us not go there today. We may visit the scene of that crime on another day.

Our residential apartment was situated at the base of the stairs which lead up to the iconic Mount Mary Church and we were frequent visitors to the church. It was a time when the Grovers and Deshpandes and Siddiquis and Iyers and Pandeys and Singhs and Kumars and Mehrotras and Banerjees, all used to visit the Church with equal devotion. It was the time when all of these used to stay together in the same building, celebrating Holi, Diwali, Eid and Christmas together. It was still a time when Hinduism, Islam and Christianity were still not threatened by each other and coexisted happily, enjoying the garba in Navratri or the Modaks of Lord Ganpati as much as the Christmas cake or the seviyan of Eid!

Going to Mount Mary Church was a frequent ritual. Racing up the 200-plus stairs with your friends, buying a candle from the vendors sitting outside, taking off your footwear, lighting the candle, sitting on the pews, being fascinated by the statues and the paintings and the overall ambience, acting like you were praying, and then rushing back down.

I happened to go back there, some time ago, after more than 30 years. While it was a trip down memory lane, one thing which struck me was all the shoes lying outside the church doors. This was such an Indian thing to do! Nowhere else in the world have I seen people taking off their shoes before entering a church. Even here, in Mount Mary Church, there were a few with their footwear still on, but the majority had taken them off outside, before entering.

While Hindus and Muslims do not enter their places of worship with their footwear, this same practice is not the norm in churches. In much of India, entering the kitchen with shoes or slippers on is not considered acceptable behaviour. In western India, in most places, people take off their footwear before entering their or others' houses, even some shops and offices. Entering a person's house or one's place of worship with footwear on, is seen as a mark of extreme disrespect. Similarly, Muslims and Sikhs never enter their shrines bare-headed. Hindu ladies (but not the menfolk) will cover their heads with their sari or dupatta when in a temple. They will do the same when they enter a gurudwara (where it is mandatory) or a church (where it is not).

Seeing all the shoes and slippers outside the church was very heartening. It was so symbolic of our Indian-ness. Here was a religion which had its origins in faraway lands and had its shrines built here and had millions of followers. These shrines were open to all and were frequented by people of all faiths. The heads bowed down and the hands joined in prayer, which asked Mother Mary for help, did not recognise any religious boundaries. The Hindu's prayer had as much fervour as the Christian's.

The shoes taken off outside the church were a way of stating that I respect your shrine and your faith as much as my own. The many Christians, by taking off their footwear outside were also silently understating the fact that their faith was just an added layer to their inherent Indian-ness.

This is the true essence of my India.

Our India.

CHAPTER FIFTEEN

THE LEAD-LINED STOMACH

It is wedding season in Gujarat. The locals and the NRIs are all marrying in droves. I have been attending back-to-back functions on a daily basis. And this morning the good old digestive tract was protesting with assorted types of discomfort.

What happened to the legendary, lead-lined stomach?

The stomach, which was trained in the squalid mess of a government Medical College mess, to digest anything and everything. After the first decade and a half of life, exposed only to wholesome home food, the introduction to the hostel mess food was a big gastronomic shock. The first tryst with the watery daal, fortified with the sweat of the hard-working Maharaj (as the cook was called) and the bits of veggies floating aimlessly in a pool of spice-infused oil made a few faint-hearted fellows wonder about their parents' true intentions in sending them to college. DNA testing was not available in those days, otherwise, I am sure that many of my fellow hostelites would have asked for paternity tests after the first few days of eating in the mess.

Those were the days when hardship was meant to be taken in one's stride. But that was 30 years ago. Today, if the Swiggy or Zomato delivery is late by even 10 minutes, the Gen X or Y or whatever is the current alphabet, behave like starved baboons in a cage.

Three decades ago, even if you wanted to complain to your parents, you had to wait till 10 PM when the STD phone call rates would become half, walk down to the PCO, stand in queue for your turn on the phone and then wind up in three minutes. This was just too much work. And anyway, most of the three minutes were spent in asking for more money and hearing reprimands for not calling home frequently enough. Also, mostly by then you had already managed an omelette, pav-bhaji, or a masala dosa from one of the many nearby roadside carts and had already moved on in life.

And then there was always Maggi; God's gift to hostelites and bachelors. The creator of Maggi noodles need not worry about his afterlife or the remaining rebirths. All those are sorted, just with the goodwill and blessings of generations of students, bachelors and unapologetic lazy buggers. While Nestle has experimented with various flavours over the decades, the good old Maggi Masala remains the evergreen favourite across generations. And those many years ago, there was no such thing as 'too much lead' and Ajinomoto wasn't even born yet. Life was so much simpler. Get Maggi, boil, eat, relax! If there was any lead in Maggi, then it would have just added to the lead lining of our stomachs.

Only the most whiny and persistent complainers would keep cribbing about the food. The rest were busy pondering the more complex problems of life like how to cover for the low attendance, avoid getting ragged by seniors, manage tickets for the latest hit movie (this was the pre-internet era, remember?), speculate whether the fleeting smile by a classmate was just a smile or a marriage proposal and trying to recall the original colour of your jeans, which had last been washed when Shah Jahan was the emperor. Food was way down on the priority list.

The stomach lining was virtually indestructible and was diligently trained in the mess to digest whatever was sent it's way. The watery daal, (which was basically boiled sweat and turmeric) and the bits of veggies scuba diving in the muddy gravies were served initially for reassurance. This was followed by the fear-inducing UFOs (unidentifiable fried objects) and the rotis with third-degree burns, which seemed to be crying for palliative care. The idlis were made of pure Kryptonite and even Superman would have broken his super teeth trying to bite into them. We later heard that the enterprising cook eventually founded his own company and made millions, by marketing his idli batter as organic concrete! The young stomach went through this rigorous training to reach the point where we could ingest and digest anything and everything.

But compared to the mess, a wedding feast is like intensive commando training for the stomach. The cold welcome drink is followed by hot soup accompanied by the starters (the commonest culprits being paneer tikka, hara bhara kabab or veg manchurian). Before the poor stomach can make sense of this Punjabi/Lucknowi/Chinese mishmash, one is already downing the pizza/pasta/dosa/ pani puri/tikki/chaat. The confused stomach now tries to commit suicide by secreting more acid and trying to drown in it. Soon thereafter, one is at the main course and the next weapons of mass indigestion include tandoori roti/ paratha/puri, chhole/kofta/paneer/daal, rice/pulao/ biryani and often mixed vegetables tortured live in frying oil on a tawa.

There is always a sad and lonely salad counter, strategically placed near the plate counter, away from the real food. But which moron goes to wedding functions to eat salads? Before the main course has had an opportunity to settle down, one is already at the dessert counter. The next phase of the onslaught is with rabdi/jalebi/gulab jamun/assorted creamy pastries/fruit cream/and assorted species of dry fruit halwa drowned in ghee. Even before these are downed, one discovers the ice cream/kulfi counter and has one for the road. By this time, the abused stomach has given up all attempts at digestion and is trying to send acid back up the esophagus to try and stop the non-stop assault. This heartburn is the final warning to stop and call it a day, or night, or evening; call it whatever you want, but please stop!

But that seems like a scene from another era. Over the years, the response to party invitations and weddings has changed from one of gustatory anticipation to that of digestive dread. The taste buds are no longer enticed by the staple food served at all such functions and the stomach cringes at the amount of acid it will have to secrete to try and destroy all the confusing stuff which will come its way The indestructible intestines are now fragile and after even a single wedding function, the whole digestive tract protests and reminds you that you aren't as young as you used to be. Also, though you may survive the acid heartburn at night, the next morning you will emit more fire from your behind than Elon Musk's SpaceX rockets.

R.I.P. The lead-lined stomach!

CHAPTER SIXTEEN

VACATION DIARIES

We are just back from our Diwali vacation.

Diwali time is a time for celebration, festivities and holidays. Diwali is also the time when Gujaratis leave their home state, and vacation in different parts of the world, where they find even more Gujaratis!

Vacations are hard work, especially if you don't want to go on group tours and want to plan your own itinerary. For group tours, all you need to do is coordinate with your fellow travellers and constantly pester your tour operator on the phone or WhatsApp. Planning and managing your own trip is like harassing yourself to get some rest!

Diwali cleaning is tiring work. Escaping from Diwali cleaning, even more so. Once I had successfully evaded all attempts to make me join in the Diwali cleaning rituals, I sat back to get some well-earned rest. It was then that I realised that I was supposed to plan a vacation this year because I had forgotten to do so the previous year and conveniently blamed it on Covid. This time I was being given constant hints that a trip to a local beach or hilltop does not count as a vacation!

Motivated by a bout of acute panic, I started searching for acceptable destinations; the operative word here being 'acceptable'. Apparently, some hill stations are too hilly, the seawater at some beaches is too salty, and some hotels aren't very homely. If, like me, you too are thinking that getting away from home is the basic premise and hotels should be 'hotelly' and not 'homely', then I strongly suggest that you not speak your thoughts out loud. Finally, there was a general consensus about the destination: we were going abroad to a beachy place.

Once the decision to go abroad was made, came the question of getting visas. Given the visa situation with the USA and Europe, the only destinations which we could aspire to go to were the ones which would give Indians a visa on arrival or an e-Visa. Since I had grandiosely decided not to avail the services of a travel agent, the onerous task of the visa application also fell on my shoulders. Visa applications are frustrating! They want to know everything about you: your dog's name, your psychiatrist's address, why a scum like you wants to visit and defile their sacred country and for how long. Anyway, since we were somewhat desperate to go, I gamely filled out the forms for all family members and checked, re-checked, re-rechecked and then cross-checked the re-re-checked forms lest a stupid spelling mistake create avoidable trouble in a foreign land.

Since the visa application required all details of entry and exit, the flight bookings had to be done first. On seeing the flight ticket fares, I felt giddy, my vision blurred, my hands started trembling and I started swaying in my seat. If my better half had been around, she would have probably diagnosed it as a stroke, pushed me onto the floor and CPR'd the hell out of me! Fortunately, she wasn't around and I booked the tickets before any further medical crisis occurred.

Next came the search for hotels. This was preceded by various advisories from various members: the resort must be centrally located but secluded, it should be away from the hustle and bustle but near the market areas, the room should be pool facing but the pool should not be room facing, the sunrise and sunset should both be visible at the same time from the balcony and other such perfectly reasonable demands. Once I entered all these criteria on Makemytrip and Booking.com, a window popped up on my laptop screen and said "Please go away and never use our website again!".

What's an annual holiday without new clothes? But these clothes brands are also strange; they keep making the clothes smaller every year. I could no longer fit into the XXL like I did last year. After I brought this to the attention of the store salespersons, they smiled and suggested that I try a larger size. They seemed to be in complete denial, refusing to acknowledge their company's fault! How rude and insensitive of them! Finally, I went for the XXXL size, but I am sure these crafty buggers will again make the clothes smaller next year and I shall have to buy the next larger size! After a couple of tiring days, we had helped 3 stores complete their annual sales targets and got 5 salespersons promoted. We were now well and truly tired and ready for a break.

The actual trip involved a 3-hour train journey to Mumbai by the stupendous Vande Bharat Express, a cab from the railway station to the airport, surprisingly with no traffic jams en route, then sampling the over-priced, late-night leftovers at the airport eateries, a 5-hour red-eye flight to our destination and another 2-hour road trip to the resort. Expectedly, by the time we reached, we were completely drained of energy.

During breakfast, the next morning, my daughter first wanted to confirm that we were actually abroad and still not in India. The hotel was teeming with Indians. The only languages heard all around were Marathi and Gujarati. The desis were swarming everywhere; the hotels, the beaches, the restaurants, the touristy places; everywhere! Surprisingly, the Bengalis were missing. It has been my observation that wherever in the world one goes, one will meet Gujarati and Bengali tourists. And I have never been disappointed. In 2019, during a professional training trip to Serbia, on a weekend off, I met a lone Bengali in the Church of Sremsi Karlovci, a small hamlet an hour away from Belgrade. He was from Mumbai, settled in Switzerland and was visiting Serbia over the weekend!

For most Indians travelling abroad, managing vegetarian food is a constant worry. The thought of having to partake of veg food cooked in the same vessels as non-veg food gives palpitations to the more finicky fellows. I have known some friends who consider it a sin to consume food of uncertain lineage and pray hard for forgiveness lest they be reborn as a spider or an octopus in the next birth. The first solution is the bag full of 'veg' food: the theplas and khakhras and namkeens and Parle-G biscuits and the 'dry fruits' and the ready-to-eat upma and poha packs and even Maggi noodles. The second solution is a universal trait which all holidaying desis display; the determined assault on the breakfast buffet! There are various reasons for this; firstly it is 'free'. Secondly, it is unlimited. Thirdly, there is a wide variety to choose from, everyone gets palatable carbs in some form or the other. Fourthly, one is not sure when, where or how the next veg meal will be; so it is best to stuff yourself so that food-wise you are sorted till dinner. And finally, we are Indians: we pile up our plates to vasool our paisa fully!

Coming back to the vacation; since we were not on a pre-planned itinerary, we enquired around, promptly activated our tourist mode and started 'touristing' all over the place. The sights which everyone was seeing, the beaches, the boat trips, the mandatory touristy activities, running all over the town, touristing away! Then we travelled to another city, checked into another hotel, and touristed even more frenetically: more cabs, more sightseeing, more beaches, more boat rides, and even more Indians!

Finally, after all the hardcore touristing, it was time to come back. The return trip comprised a day flight to Mumbai and a long road trip back to Surat, first through the rush hour Mumbai traffic followed by a few hours on the highway. The highway drive was interrupted by loo breaks, and food breaks, followed by nausea and vomiting breaks. Finally, we reached home at midnight, after an arduous 16-hour journey, exhausted and completely drained.

The next day, after settling in, getting the laundry done, stocking up on the food, checking homework, and doing the usual stuff of domesticity, we were back to our original selves: at home, overworked and exhausted. And we hadn't even restarted work yet!

We would have readily left for another holiday, but vacations are just too tiring!

CHAPTER SEVENTEEN

WHEN WILL I BE MYSELF?

I sit and try to listen to the patient's complaints with a suitable amount of interest and empathy. He has a vague discomfort in some unspecified region, which crops up at uncertain intervals and disturbs his sleep. He has been to seventy five doctors previously and nobody could find anything wrong with him. His problem does not interest me in the least, today. I just want him to stop talking, get up and go away.

I have had a fight with my spouse. All couples fight, mostly over stupid things. But today's fight was a King Kong vs Godzilla level engagement. Needless to say, neither of us came out happy or satisfied. I am sure that my spouse, like me, is also battling a tsunami of emotions since the morning.

I want to sit alone in a room and shut out the world.

I want to ponder over what went wrong.

I want to sit and cry.

But I can't.

I have to reach my clinic; patients are waiting. People have booked appointments to meet me, to get my help in solving their problems. Not reaching on time is unprofessional. Cancelling appointments for something as inconsequential as a domestic tiff is unpardonable. So I have to sit and talk to patients, listen to them and try to solve their problems, even though it may be the last thing which I want to do. I have to put myself, my problems, my feelings aside and behave professionally.

This isn't something new. It has been going on ever since childhood.

Throughout childhood, I studied and performed well in exams. Even when I wanted to skip homework and play or read comic books, I could never do so. I was a model student, I couldn't behave like the 'bad' students. As I grew up, it was assumed that I would take up either medicine or engineering as a career; that's what the 'good' students did. Career options other than medicine and engineering were considered sub-par for bright students, in those days. Going by how much I have to act normal nowadays. I would have made a reasonable actor.

After joining Medical College, for a short while I discovered who I really was, but even here, I couldn't be myself. I had to be smart and witty in front of the opposite sex. I had to be adequately cool and sporting with my friends. I had to be sincere and hardworking for my teachers (and for my scores). Thankfully, after finishing MBBS, post-graduation started almost immediately, otherwise, I would have had to act knowledgeable in front of my parents and relatives. Only a freshly qualified MBBS graduate knows what Socrates meant when he said "I only know that I know nothing".

During post-graduation, I initially felt like an untrained and unarmed soldier sent to fight on the front lines. But since you are the first point of contact with the patient, you have to keep up the facade and act as if you really know what you are doing. As time passed, the confidence became somewhat more genuine, but the feudal postgraduate training system did not allow you to oppose even grossly wrong decisions, if they were made by your seniors. Any dissidence and you could become persona non grata immediately. Everyone in the medical profession everyone knows that one does not need to be knowledgeable to harass postgraduates during ward rounds or clinics. After finally finishing training, when I started practising, I again had to act confident and sound knowledgeable. It was the same old story all over again.

On the personal front, the closest to when I could be myself was in the company of friends. Slowly the friends drifted away and settled in faraway places and moved on in life. The friendships still remain, but now it is mostly over video calls, and almost always, everyone is in a hurry to disconnect and go to attend to some commitment.

As a son, I always had to put up a brave face. Even when your mother is diagnosed with cancer or your father with heart disease requiring bypass surgery, you have to remain unruffled and keep reassuring everyone that everything will be fine. All this, when you are constantly thinking about all the surgical complications which can occur and everything which can go wrong. But I am not allowed that liberty. The man of the house has to remain strong; or at least, appear strong.

As a spouse, there was never enough time together during post-graduation. Now when we were trying to establish our practice, there was even less time spent together. Even with your spouse, you have to remain calm and collected and give the impression that you are in control, and capable of solving any problems which life throws at you. All this, when you may be losing sleep over a surgical complication in a patient or the state of your finances, or maybe you have been threatened with a lawsuit but don't want to add to your spouse's troubles.

It is said that office problems should stay in the office and should not be brought home. But in today's connected world, that is rarely possible. Hospital problems never stay restricted to the hospital and the office follows you home every day. The Boss wants the status of your project no matter what time you finish or the overseas client may only be available at night due to the time lag. Work From Home has legitimised the intrusion of your office and your profession into your home. And even when we are physically at the workplace, we have to maintain our professionalism. We may have just faced the Boss' anger or maybe missed a promotion. But we have to put away our own emotions and fears and keep smiling for the world. And in doing so, we often forget who we really are.

Even if my child is sick at home, I have to be at my professional best when I am with my patients. Or if I am having a frustratingly difficult time with my teenage kid, I cannot allow that to reflect in my behaviour or my decision-making. People's lives are at stake. Whatever happens, I have to maintain the aura of infallibility.

We all have to do that every day at our workplaces.

I have almost forgotten who I am.

I have been everything; a son, a spouse, a friend, a parent, a student, a teacher, and a clinician.

But when will I be myself?

CHAPTER EIGHTEEN

SO HELP ME GOD!

Life was becoming like a cup of tea which had gone cold. I still wanted to have it, but not in its present state. I could heat it up on a stove or microwave it, but the will and energy to do that were both missing. The midlife crisis was manifesting in a weirdly lethargic way. I decided I needed help and turned to God. But His corporate policies seem to have changed over the years.

When we were kids, we were taught that God had sent us to help others. I once asked my Moral Science teacher that if we were here to help others, then what were the other, lazy buggers here for? Obviously, the teacher did not know the answer and I was sternly told to keep my opinion to myself and not ask such rude questions.

Over the years, the Big Boss seems to have become either overloaded with work or plain lethargic. Because, now God helps only those who help themselves. This policy is confusing because if one were able to help oneself, then one would not be asking God and once already self-helped, one would then not be in need of further help. So basically this God person set up a blind loop algorithm and Himself escaped from all responsibility; a cunning trick used by mid-level managers and politicians!

But anyway, the cold tea in the gloomy cup of life badly needed to be heated, so I decided to help myself. And promptly set about buying self-help books and also asking the omniscient Google for 'self-help' tips.

Dr Abdul Kalam once said "Dreams are not what you see while sleeping, they are something that do not let you sleep". But the only thing not letting me sleep for the last so many weeks was Netflix. Since I was wasting most of my time watching mindless series on Netflix and Prime Video, I was not dreaming. And since I wasn't dreaming, I had no dreams to chase. Having nothing else to do, I could now binge-watch the next season of "Kahani Palace Palace Ki" or "Kyonki Kween Bhi Kabhi Bahu Thi" without guilt. I hear the bahu is actually an undercover Naagin and Ekta Kapoor is planning to bring back the Queen; with a rebirth to keep the saas bahu drama going!

According to Google, someone called Schuller said "Problems are not stop signs, they are guidelines". My guidelines seem to be written in an unknown language which I cannot understand. Apparently, Google can, because when I tried using Google Translate to decipher what my problems were telling me, Google tried to divert my attention by showing me funny cat videos. And now my mobile phone is on antidepressants.

Most motivational books inevitably harp upon the fact that Google, Microsoft and Disney, all started in a garage. So I went in search of one in my residential complex. Alas, leave alone a garage, there wasn't even enough parking space for the bikes and scooters in the building compound and even now half of the cars had to be parked on the road outside the complex. This garage thing wasn't going to work in India. I had to try something else.

Another common feature was that all these fellows who made it big, used to work hard and mostly sleep in the office. Now, being a surgeon, the only option available was to stay back and sleep in the hospital and I proceeded to do just that. However, by midnight, I was terrified by the thought that I might wake up in the morning and find a kidney or a testicle missing and promptly escaped to the safety of my own bed in my garage-less apartment.

Google also told me that "Inspiration does exist, but it must find you working." Now I have been working fairly hard for a long time. However, all surgical work is done in sterile operation theatres where entry is strictly restricted. So I now think that inspiration must have come sometime when I was operating and must not have been allowed into the operating room by the staff nurses. Taking a cue from time and tide, which wait for no man, inspiration also decided that it would also not wait for me and probably went to look for someone working in a garage, which is so much easier to enter.

Another wise man said, "Your time is limited, so don't waste it living someone else's life". Here I was finding it difficult to live my own life, let alone someone else's life. If I tried to live someone else's life, I have no doubt that I would make it so boring and uninteresting that compared to it, sitting and meditating in a cave in the Himalayas would look like the action in an Avengers movie. So having pity on the poor sod, I dropped the idea of living his life. Which brought me back to the cold tea in the metaphorical cup.

One more wise idiot stated, "The way to get started is to quit talking and begin doing". So I stopped talking to my wife but couldn't recall what it was that I had wanted to do in the first place. Also, my wife did not stop talking to me.

Needless to say, this approach did not end well for me.

A multitude of people ranging from Shakespeare to Ratan Tata to my neighbour's grand uncle's maternal aunt seem to have said, "If you can think it, you can do it". Henry Ford even said that the opposite was also true. I proved them all wrong!

I thought it.

I couldn't do it.

When life cools your tea, maybe you should add some ice and have iced tea

CHAPTER NINETEEN

COLLEGE REUNION: THE PLANNING

It has been 30 years since we joined college. Like every year, this year too, around the same time, there is a clamour for a reunion on the college Whatsapp group. The active and interested members, who plan and execute the reunion every time are often in the minority. Then there are those who keep saying yes to everything, don't help in the planning and invariably disappear in the end. The last group consists of the complainers and objectors; they will find fault with everything, the dates, the venue, the past, the present and the future.

Then the active members get charged up and start planning. Generally, it is the same few members who plan and organise the event every time. The first hurdle is the date; the NRIs are available only in December. But it is time for the pre-Boards or term exams at that time. So then sometime in October? Some other members' kids have unit tests, coaching classes or some other exams. What about September? Ohh there are too many medical conferences in September so....

The summer months are too hot, the monsoons too wet and the winters too exam-infested. After excluding all the months of the year, it is finally decided that the meeting will be in December because ultimately it is the same people who come to the reunions every time and they will come in whichever month it is planned. So what's wrong with December?

Then comes the date. Early December is not acceptable to anyone for some reason. Mid-December is the wedding season and no hotels will be available around Christmas and New Year. Mid-December is decided upon and members are politely told to choose between obscure relatives at a boring ceremony or old college time friends who are now as bald and obese as you are. There is always one chap who will protest the selected date. He really wants to attend but his aunt's sister's cousin's neighbour's stepfather's grandson is getting married and he just has to attend because he is very close to his uncle's brother's stepdaughter. This is often the same fellow who appears very keen to reunite but objects to every date as he has some function to attend. Since he got the dates changed three times in the past and then finally did not show up at any event, his objections are given the same importance as traffic signals on Indian roads.

The next step is the venue. The first suggestion is always to meet in the city where we all studied purely for nostalgic reasons. This is met with enthusiasm by some and opposition by many. It's too far away from where most of the batch stays now, too much time will be spent travelling, we met here last time too, and the local guys will keep running away to attend to emergencies. The reasons proffered are many and varied. The ones complaining are also the fellows who either don't come or who don't mix up with the rest and stay in their own groups, away from the rest. Again the venue is decided keeping in mind the convenience of the most number of numbers, even though everyone knows that the ones creating a fuss will fall ill, create a family emergency or maybe kill a relative to avoid attending.

While the active planners start scouting and finalising the venue, in the background, some Track 2 diplomacy always goes on. One or two active members take it upon themselves to call everyone and request them to join because it will be fun and so on. After listening to some strange excuses and some outright rude responses, the initial enthusiasm to call up people wears off. WTH! It's not my daughter's wedding, is it? Whoever wants to come will come! And if these rude and unpleasant fellows don't come, well, all the better!

Meanwhile, the planning for the actual event begins. There are demands for karaoke, Antakshari, dumb charades, a DJ, games for the wives and kids, a swimming pool, a magic show, a bunker to protect against a nuclear bomb attack and a police battalion to provide security. In addition, Salman Khan has to get married, Barack Obama must come and sing a Hindi song and Baba Ramdev has to do the bhangra. Ultimately the same old people take responsibility for organising the same old games and the same old event manager is hired to embarrass the middle-aged crowd in newer and more innovative ways.

CHAPTER TWENTY

COLLEGE REUNION: THE BIG DAY

Finally, the big day arrives and everyone starts trickling into the designated venue. There is always a banner, the sole purpose of which is to serve as a background for group photos. There is a lot of hugging and back-slapping as old friends meet. The hairlines have receded further, and the bald patches and bellies are bigger. While the bald patches are occasionally pointed to and made fun of, the bulging waistlines are mostly accepted as part of ageing.

It has been my observation that most ladies mature gracefully while most men don't mature at all.

As more people join, the atmosphere becomes festive and the fun and games begin.

A couple of the active members initiate the ice breaking with the mandatory 'short' speech. The old college alliances form again and people migrate to their old groups. Antakshari is the default setting for starting off any and every meeting and the next 2 hours are full of cacophony, loud and off key songs, wrong tries, shouting, mike snatching and laughter.

The event manager (EM) has set up his or her stuff by now and is all eager to start with the 'games'. The games typically involve balloons, glasses of water, ribbons, group activities and any activity which can make you look stupid. After the initial reluctance, the mood lightens, the inhibitions drop and everyone seems to be having fun. Again there are always a few moody fellows who have to be pulled into the arena every time. By the time it's time for a break, the EM is more tired than the participants. After the tea break, the old friends are all charged up and by the end of the session, the EM is literally begging for mercy and asking to go home before he or she dies of exhaustion. The session breaks till dinner after which is the most awaited event, the 'DJ' session.

The break is utilised differently by the men and the women. While the ladies will freshen up, change and get all decked up for the event, the men have only one question: "In which room is the liquor?". Being a 'dry' state, alcohol cannot be consumed publicly. But that is never really a deterrent. There are always a couple of guys who know exactly how and where to get the booze from, irrespective of the city or town. And these fellows will have arranged for all sorts of alcohol well in advance. The guys all migrate to the drinks room, even the non-drinkers who don't want to be left out of that unique male bonding which occurs over alcohol.

After a few drinks and a lot of bawdy humour, it's time for the DJ event. By now, some latecomers have also joined and there is some more hugging and back-slapping. The DJ starts off with some slow numbers as the members settle in. Seeing the middle-aged crowd, he puts up some slow 90s numbers, which the crowd likes. To test the waters, he puts on a dance number and a few people get on the floor. They are not the real dancer types but they know that no one will start till someone else does. Then they drag other reluctant ones. Soon the dance floor is a free-for-all area. Everyone is suddenly 30 years younger and moving uninhibited, with no fear of being judged. The fat guys groove as enthusiastically as the bald ones. No one is bothered about who is moving which body part, as long as everyone is having fun.

These guys don't judge you. They are the ones who stayed with you in the hostel and who have seen you moving around in your dirty and torn underwear. They lent you money and their motorcycle, for your first date. They cared for you when you were down with malaria. They woke you up during exams, with a cup of tea. They marked your proxy attendance when you were asleep in your room. They definitely don't judge you.

The better dancers try choreographed moves of Bollywood movie songs but the charged crowd follows no rules. After an hour, the DJ is seriously scared that someone will soon have a heart attack and collapse and tries to play a slow song to decrease the tempo. One of the spirited guys goes and says something extremely rude in his ear, possibly referring to certain assorted body parts. The DJ turns visibly red with embarrassment and switches back to the dance numbers thinking "Let them die dancing, why should I care?".

The hotel or resort staff turn up at 11 p.m. to announce that the time is over. The spirited guy is sent to remind them about various assorted body parts and what to do with them and they retreat fearfully. The DJ is now tired and so is the crowd, but nobody is ready to acknowledge that they are older. And fatter. And dead tired. So the music goes on for another 30 minutes till everyone is ready to collapse right there. Somehow the last song before winding up at every such event is a fast-paced Bhangra number which has everyone back on their feet. One last time. Everyone joins in; not sure of when there will be a next time.

Finally, the DJ leaves and everyone keeps sitting around chatting, less because they want to, but more because no one wants to walk back to their rooms. After some time, one brave soul after another troop back to their rooms, knees hurting, backs paining and shoulders sore. It is discovered that one member has a strip of analgesics and everyone lines up at his door for a pill, till his stock runs out.

Everyone promises to be up early the next morning for another chat session.

Other than some compulsive early risers, nobody wakes up! Most drag themselves out of bed just because the breakfast timings are going to get over. Over breakfast, people share fond memories of the previous night's antics and the resulting aches and pains which are still troubling them. While everyone would like to sit back and chat away, refreshing memories and getting all nostalgic, everyone has responsibilities to get back to. Everyone comes together in the foyer or reception and there is another round of hugging and goodbyes with earnest promises to keep in touch which will soon be forgotten in the daily grind of life.

The reception is soon flooded with people checking out and after more byes and waves, the few who had actually planned everything are left behind. After the hotel bills are all settled, the final group also disperses.

Reunions are fun. One day, you are a senior doctor; all serious and professional and the very next day, you are a completely different personality. At least for those few hours spent with old friends, you are yourself. If any of your patients see your antics during reunions, they may never come back to you again. Some may even doubt their own sanity but will never risk consulting a Psychiatrist, because he may also be acting similarly at his reunions.

The inevitable chats comprise stories of the golden olden days, the love stories, the secret crushes, the bunked classes, the movies seen by skipping lectures, the anecdotes of hostel life, the idiosyncrasies of teachers, and the annoying toppers who everyone wants to irritate but who somehow never come for reunions. You become 30 years younger, if just for a day. And leave with a heavy heart, because in your heart you know that this was just an escape from reality.

Life is waiting, with all its challenges.

Waiting for you to return.

CHAPTER TWENTY-ONE

SPEED BREAKERS, FLYOVERS & METROS

Urban planning in India may appear very complicated, but is actually very simple.

Where the traffic is fast, make a speed breaker.

Where the traffic is slow, build a flyover.

And, when everything is working well, plan a Metro and dig up everything.

What is it with Indians and speed breakers? Making speed breakers is like the official pastime of Municipalities in India. India must have the highest number of speed breakers per citizen and per kilometre of road, compared to any other country in the world.

Speed breakers are primarily meant to deter morons from overspeeding in danger zones like schools and hospitals or to slow them down near crossings and turns, to prevent pedestrians and cyclists from being run over. However, some of them exist just because some irritable and hypersensitive Uncles in some Housing Society decided so.

Speed breakers are symbolic of a lot of what is wrong with us as a society. If you can't solve a problem, we create a solution which is almost as problematic as the original problem. Indians have mastered the fine art of designing and building speedbreakers. Offhand, I can recall five types.

The first type, the ideal one, is smoothly rounded, neither too high nor too low, enough to slow you down without breaking your back. Like common sense, this one is extremely rare to find.

The second is the single, small bumpy strip, often made of black and yellow plastic. This is meant to give you a strong jerk, enough to send a warning but not cause any real damage. These ones are generally targeted at cyclists, bikers and scooterists. While they may just angrily jolt speeding cars, they hold the potential to break a speeding scooter's spine and the rider's will. People slow down for these more to prevent damage to their bikes than due to any great sense of civic responsibility. These ones are often adorned with needless reflectors and found within residential complexes to protect residents from the enemy within.

The third type is the nearly flat, apologetic breaker. This one was put in half-heartedly by a municipality team which was getting late for lunch. These speed breakers are a minor inconvenience which no one bothers about. These breakers are like a politician's election promises, they offer a solution where no problem existed to begin with.

The fourth type is the so-called 'rumble strip'; some eight or ten small bumpy ones of the first variety placed one after the other. Going even slowly over these can give you motion sickness and going over them with any speed can lead to a broken chassis, create a hernia, shake out any evil spirits residing within you and later cause nightmares which Sigmund Freud would find difficult to interpret.

The last in the series is the big, arrogant mound which competes with the Sardar Sarovar dam in its height. The sole purpose of these perverted bumps seems to be to scrape the delicate bottoms of as many passing cars as they can. No matter what a driver tries, to avoid these lusty deviants, the perverted breakers manage to slap the car's bottom.

Once enough speed breakers have been built to create traffic jams, we then solve the problem by constructing flyovers. This is another typical Indian trait; whenever confronted with a significant problem, just look away and change your path, and maybe the problem will go away. Once a flyover is built, what happens below is none of your problem. As long as we can speed away on our bikes or in our cars, the world below the flyover may as well not exist. Poverty, molestation, drugs, murders, everything is acceptable as long as it stays below the flyover and doesn't disturb the traffic above.

It is only when the flyover is closed for repairs, that we realize that there exists a world below; a world where real people live. Because then we have to drive our precious vehicles on the road below the hallowed flyover; our swanky sedans and our obnoxious SUVs, on the stinky, shitty roads in the smelly areas inhabited by nameless and faceless people. If a flyover is closed, the government should provide helicopters to its citizens so that they do not have to hobnob with these strange, sad-looking people who exist in this dirty world below. Forcing us to interact with such creatures is demeaning and a violation of our fundamental rights. Thank God, we won't have to come down into this filth once the flyover reopens!

And finally, when everything seems to be working smoothly, the civic authorities decide that it's time for a rejig and plan a Metro. The Metro construction teams swoop down on all the unlucky roads and localities and dig up everything; water pipes, gas lines, drainage pipes, electrical cables, everything. They leave absolutely nothing to chance. They come, they block roads, they dig, they disappear. The poor commuters who have to take new diversions every day to reach work or home or anywhere, keep wondering when the Metro pillars will appear. But like the storylines of Indian TV serials, there is just a pointless prolongation, with no progress. A child entering Nursery or KG may be lucky if the Metro is up and running by the time he finishes college. And he will in turn father a child, who will want his own vehicle and will not use the Metro. To this thankless progeny, he will fondly narrate tales of how he had to climb over mountains of dirt to reach school and swim back via the sewer line to reach home because the Metro workers had blocked all the roads.

Finally, a few generations later, when the Metro is up and running, the drainage guys will come and dig up the road. In the process, they will cut some electric cables, which will be discovered after they have left. The electricity department people will then dig up the road to repair their cables but drill through a water pipeline. By the time the water supply has been restored, the monsoons will have started, and the rains will just wash away whatever remains of the road. The PWD team will rebuild the road halfheartedly and will have just left when the Telecom department fellows come back to dig up everything once again. If you try to convince them that nobody uses landlines any more, they get even more riled up and will exchange your drinking water and sewer lines. To investigate this, the Waterworks teams will come and again dig up everything.

Finally, when everything seems to have settled down, and life is again going smoothly, one fine day, the Corporation teams will come and construct a speed breaker to slow down the traffic.

CHAPTER TWENTY-TWO

A HANDFUL OF DUST

The basic tenet of the Bhagavad Gita is to do one's duty.

But what is our duty?

What are we here for?

From a purely scientific perspective, we are born, we grow older, we reproduce and then we die. Biologically, that is all we are intended to do.

That is what all life forms do: Exist, reproduce, and then stop existing.

But aren't we humans supposed to be an evolved life form? Our intellect lets us think about abstract things, things which do not exist physically. We try to find meaning in our existence. And that is what makes us superior to other life forms (or so we think). Elephants don't look up at the sky and wonder about the stars. Cows don't fight over politics. Lizards don't discuss the latest movies or the degradation of the education system. We do! Because we can. Because we think!

And logically we come around to thinking about the reason for our existence, why we are here.

What is our raison d'etre?

What is our duty?

What is it, that we live to achieve?

After he had finished writing "The History Of The Sikhs", noted author Khushwant Singh wrote at the end: "Opus Exegii"; meaning 'My work is done'. That he went on to become a much bigger personality thereafter is a different matter. Some people are evidently born to fulfil a particular destiny in their lives. Mother Teresa existed to help the unwanted. Jagjit Singh and Ghulam Ali were created to sing ghazals. Tendulkar was born to bat. But the purpose of life isn't so evident for many of us.

In the hugely underrated masterpiece of a movie 'Sonchiriya', the protagonist (played by the late Sushant Singh Rajput) is a dacoit (or rebel, as the dacoits call themselves). Throughout the movie, he keeps asking his fellow outlaw, Vakil (played by the talented Ranvir Shorey) what their duty is, what they exist for. His constant refrain is "The duty of policemen is to kill rebels. But what is the duty of a rebel"? The whole story revolves around the gang of bandits finding their raison d'etre and laying down their lives for it.

What is that cause, that aim which one could die for? Or more precisely, what is that goal which one would want to live for? What is our duty in life?

Why is this simple question so difficult to answer?

A doctor's duty is first and foremost the well-being of his patients, while that of a parent is that of his or her child. An architect has a duty to model a safe but elegant structure while fulfilling his client's requirements. A teacher's duty is to teach, and that of a sportsman may be to perform for his team, club or country. A pilot's duty is the safety of his passengers, crew and aircraft.

Why is it so difficult for us to recognise our mission in life? How many of us really know what our mission in life is?

Most of us have no idea why we exist and what we live for. What most of us indulge in is a daily drudgery where we go to work, fulfil our responsibilities and come back home, to fulfil more responsibilities. It is not that we don't like our work or we don't work sincerely. But there is a difference between your work and your passion. And how many of us can really profess to say that our work is our passion, for which we would be ready to sacrifice everything?

A surgeon loves to operate, an architect likes designing buildings and a cricketer loves to play. But that does not make it their mission in life. Most of us look to our work as a means of livelihood (and rightfully so) but not much more than that. But how many of us would do things just out of interest? How many teachers would teach for the sake of teaching? How many sportsmen would continue playing if there was no money to be made? A doctor who can't earn from his practice will soon be looking for other gainful employment. So would a lawyer. The list is endless.

That brings us to our responsibilities. We are burdened with responsibilities, as sons or daughters, as parents, as professionals, as employees, and as friends. Every day we live a life of multiple identities, each with its own burdens. And most responsibilities need time and importantly, money, to be fulfilled. Which ties us down to our daily routines, our jobs, and our professions.

After a lifetime of slogging, what most of us will have to show for will be children who have been brought up and are grown-ups, independent and well-settled. This is the same thing which lesser evolved species also achieve but without all the hoopla and the fragile egos.

Animals live, and so do we (but we probably do it with more flair).

Animals reproduce, and so do we (again with more flourish).

Animals rear their kids till they become capable of surviving independently, and so do we (but with infinitely more complications in the process).

Animals die, and so do we (but with many more regrets).

Then where does the difference lie?

The difference lies in us having a duty, a mission and devoting our lives to it.

Which brings us back to the question of how many of us really know what our duty is.

The reason for someone's existence cannot be just earning more money, buying more land or becoming CEO. Neither should it be just raising children. One's deeds and work must be such that they make a difference to someone's life, to society, and to humanity.

A graceful monument envisioned by a visionary architect and brought to life by passionate engineers, a work of art which will be appreciated by future generations, a book which leaves a mark, students who were inspired by you, some people who did not have to sleep hungry because of you, a poor boy whose education you sponsored, the ways and deeds can be infinite.

What will be our biggest regret on our deathbeds? Will we be unhappy that we did not earn more money or make a bigger house? Or will we be sadder that we have nothing substantial to show for a lifetime of hard work? Do we really want to look back at our lives and regret that we could not do our duty? Because we never realised what our duty was?

Bahadurshah Zafar was the last Emperor of the Mughal dynasty and was rendered completely powerless and exiled from Delhi by the British. Towards the end of his days, he wrote this couplet lamenting his insignificance:

"Na kisi ki aankh ka noor hoon, na kisi ke dil ka karaar hoon

Jo kisi ke kaam na aa sakaa, main woh ek musht-e-gubaar hoon"

(Neither am I the apple of anyone's eye nor am I loved or desired,

I am like that handful of dust, which is of no use to anyone)

There is still time.

Let us make a small difference.

Let us make our lives count for something.

Let us not end our lives feeling like a handful of dust.

CHAPTER TWENTY-THREE

GROAN UPS

Definition: Adults who are not 'cool' and are constantly in a state of self-inflicted responsibility.

Most children dream of becoming older and being able to do 'grown-up' stuff.

My daughters do not want to grow up.

And they have very specific reasons for not wanting to do so.

They keep reminding me that I have no 'chill' in life. I am the typical grown-up; always busy, mostly serious and always worried about something or the other. Also, as per them, I lose more points because I don't savour ice creams. I actually love ice cream, but it has too many calories. If my dietician were to find out that I had cheated and had an ice cream, she would develop a stroke and I fear that my gym trainer (who has the body and the brains of a gorilla) may become angry and bash my head in with a dumbbell. Sorry, I can't take that risk. So avoiding ice cream is more like a social service. The dietician has kids waiting at home and the gym trainer may be taken back to the zoo if he becomes violent.

My kids just don't understand.

As for being worried, the girls are mistaken. I am not worried about anything. In fact, I want them to become independent and so, don't interfere in their lives at all. Sometimes I shout at them for not waking up on time, not combing their hair, not finishing homework on time, missing the school bus, not getting enough marks and spending too much time on their phones. But that is because they need to be disciplined and competitive. And I read a message on Whatsapp, by a senior and famous doctor from AIIMS, that spending too much time on social media is not good. It can lead to influenza, intoxication, infertility, insanity, incontinence and cancer. I am really worried about the incontinence part.

They also complain that I am always serious and not fun to be around. That is not so. I am a happy fellow and don't complain much. But a man has a right to speak up when that idiot of a fielder drops a catch (he must have bribed the selectors to get on the team). Also, a toddler can bat better than that oaf they send in, to open every time. Bloody idiots! What are these nincompoops being paid for? Buggers are getting easy money. Pukka, they must be goofing off in the evenings and doing parties and stuff instead of practising.

Where were we?

Yes! As I said, I don't complain much about anything. There are so many things in life to be thankful for. Just like there are so many taxes to be paid. Taxes, taxes, taxes, all the government does is increase the taxes. It's as if I work only to pay taxes. And what do I get in return; just look at the quality of the roads, the railways, and the gardens. Everywhere there is corruption. No one wants to work. Everyone just wants to make quick money. And here I keep slogging for what? Just to pay these stupid taxes! Coming back to my point, as I was saying, I really don't complain much.

And I am really not all that busy either. They just exaggerate things. Just because I have missed the parent-teacher meetings for the last 4 years, or have never reached their birthday parties in time or last saw them awake about 3 days ago, doesn't mean that I am too busy for my family. The next time they are awake when I am at home, I'll have a word with them. I would have done it today, but there is too much work pending.

They also say that I am hyper-competitive. I cannot enjoy fun and games. They cannot be more wrong. But then they got only 99.9% marks in their final exams. Can you believe that? How can you not get the remaining 0.1%? With this score, the rest of the 99.9 marks are a total waste. Who scores 99.9% marks? Only stupid idiots! And when I told them this, they felt unnecessarily offended and started crying. Behaving like absolute losers.

Like the time when one of them participated in the 400-meter race; she won the gold. And when I told her that it was not enough to just win a gold and that she should have broken the World record, or at least the Olympic record, she started crying and saying that I didn't appreciate any of her achievements. Unnecessary drama, I say. What's the point of just winning? Not breaking any records is as good as losing!

And the younger one was offended when I was trying to cheer her up during her race. She also won, but she did not like the fact that I had jumped into the ground and was running along and shouting at her for being as slow as a tortoise. She was also embarrassed by the fact that I called their Sports Teacher a lazy nincompoop and got into a fight with the staff who were trying to send me back into the stands. What's the use of so much ground if you don't even allow anyone to run on it and she should be proud of me, it took four of them to pin me down. And two of them cried when I bit them! Losers! Sissies!

I think I may be beginning to understand what the problem is.

I think they don't mind being grown-ups.

Maybe they just don't want to become groan-ups!

CHAPTER TWENTY-FOUR

YOGA CLASS

I finally joined Yoga Class. After years and years of thinking, planning, researching and then some more planning, I finally enrolled in a local Yoga group. Of course, it did require a bit of nudging by my better half; a lot of it actually. But like a Vogon, she convinced me that resistance was futile and like Arthur Dent, I surrendered. Anyway, yoga was supposed to be gentle and relaxing.

The first step was preparing for the class. Now, compared to gymming, prepping for yoga is simpler; you don't need special shoes, gym gloves, water bottles, napkins, wrist bands, knee braces, BCAA or assorted protein powders. But I still had to get proper yoga-compatible clothes, a yoga mat and a really loud alarm clock. I asked the shopkeeper if he had some motivation which I could buy. He muttered something rude under his breath and stared at me oddly. I think that they did not have it in stock.

I reached there a few minutes late on the first day, which should be perfectly acceptable by Indian standards. Apparently, it wasn't. When I reached, the initial invocation was going on. The 'Om' reverberating through the hall was mesmerizing. I imagined myself in a temple in Rishikesh. If I were a foreigner, I would probably have donated all my wealth and settled down in India, the land of spirituality. Unfortunately, I was already settled in India.

Anyway, I started attending regularly with sufficient enthusiasm. Among the first things I noticed was that the class consisted mainly of middle-aged people and the women outnumbered the men. The men were mostly middle-aged like me. There were a couple of young girls, probably in their teens. But there were no teenage boys. And the only guys in their 20s and 30s were the ones who came along with their wives. No full-blooded teenage boy or young male can be coaxed or threatened to join a yoga class, it's just too uncool. If by chance a teenager has a heart attack outside a yoga class, he will probably drag himself to a nearby gym and collapse there, rather than risk his reputation being seen around a yoga class.

Even early in the morning, the women were well groomed and proper in their attire with yoga pants and yoga shirts and yoga mats and yoga etiquette. The men, on the other hand, looked mostly like they had just stepped out of bed and come to class directly, in their night clothes. Also, the sincere ones always clustered together and motivated each other. Lazy and stiff fellows like me would look around for other lazy fellows who found it difficult to bend and stretch and we would invariably band together and console each other when we couldn't do much (which was pretty much most of the time).

The yoga teachers would instruct us to start with ardhjdgtythsdafhj-asan. By the time I was getting the pronunciation correct, the rest of the class would be done and ready for the next pose. I feel the names are kept difficult for a purpose. They are part of the exercise. The tongue has to do about 13 different asanas just to pronounce them correctly. Then we would do bghtyjdesutyhffg-asan. Even after a few months, I would pretty much be lagging a few seconds behind the class so that I could try and copy what the others were doing. And as a matter of habit since my primary school days, I always stood behind everyone. Once a last-bencher, always a last-bencher.

Often, when we got the instruction to do something like wriyhTh-asan, the teacher would come up to me in exasperation and ask me "What do you think you are doing"? And I would say "wriyhth-asan"? "No! It's wriyhTh-asan! With a capital 'T'. Not wriyhth-asan. wriyhth-asan is the three-legged lion asan and you are doing wriyhTh-asan, which is the one-eyed, retarded monkey asan!"

Oops!

Other times it would go like this: "Raise your right arm up. Now raise your left arm up. Pull upwards". And it would bring back fond memories of school and I would go into a trance. By the time everyone else had finished the rest of the asan, I would keep standing with my hands up in the air, smiling like an idiot. Exactly like school days!

One asan entailed bending forwards and trying to touch the floor, without bending your knees. I am about as flexible as a bamboo and the best I could manage after a lot of struggle was to reach somewhere around my knees. To avoid being chastised, I cheated and bent my knees after which my hands could just reach to my knees. The ever-observant yoga teacher noticed this, came up behind me silently and tried to straighten my legs. My ample belly makes for a very high centre of gravity and with this manoeuvre, I tipped right over, straight into the butt of the poor, unsuspecting fellow in front of me, who in turn also fell forwards. This set off a cascade and in a few seconds there was total chaos and my whole row was sprawled on the floor in a sea of flailing arms and feet. In a gym, there would have been some very colourful language also, but it wasn't so in yoga class. Thank God for small mercies. Here everyone just did a Namaste and went back to try and lick their knees.

And then there were these exotic asans, where the instructions would go like: "Stand straight. Lift your buttocks. Lift your buttocks. Lift. Lift. Lift''. And the sincere student that I was, I lifted and lifted till my butt reached my head and the rest of my body became confused about which of these was the part with the brain. However, it was soon apparent that interchanging the two wouldn't make much of a difference.

Finally, there were the question-answer sessions at the end where the teachers would ask questions like: "How did you feel after sfgsgfrriuruy-asan"? Apparently, 'tired' and 'frustrated' were not the correct answers. Then they would ask "How was the thought process during the sfgsgfrriuruy-asan"? And the sincere members would respond something like "I felt that my mind was aligned with my body" or "I was more aware of contact with my inner self". My answer "I was confused and clueless' was not appreciated. And "During the sfgsgfrriuruy-asan what were you thinking about"?. The answer to this question was expected to be "I was thinking about and feeling the energy flowing from my ugly toes to my empty skull". Again, my answer that I was thinking about aloo parathas and jalebis was not found to be acceptable.

But I improved with time.

Now I can actually bend forward without toppling over and my hands reach up to my knees, my back is now more flexible (somewhat like a bent bamboo).

Now, I can also say "I felt that the focus of my brain was on the energy being released by the positive vibes generated by the intense mind-calming influence of the asan" with a straight face, without laughing out loud.

Namaste!

CHAPTER TWENTY-FIVE

DIET HARD

In general fat guys know a lot about dieting and have tried myriad diets over the years, before grudgingly accepting defeat in the battle of the bulge. Mediterranean, Subterranean, Caveman, Batman, Superman; you name it and we have tried the diet. And we are always ready to give it a try, once more..... I once had the good fortune of meeting Dr Jagannath Dixit during a conference where we were both speakers. He had been allotted a full hour to illuminate us on what he is best known for: The Dixit Diet, or more accurately, The Dixit Lifestyle. I had 12 minutes to talk about what I was good at being fat and jolly! Dr Dixit is a soft-spoken and unassuming gentleman and is very passionate about and committed to his cause. His videos are freely available on YouTube and are immensely popular. You should see them and will then understand that their popularity is well deserved. He came over to me and personally suggested that I follow his method for a few months and see.

The basics are as follows:

Eat only twice a day.

Eat only when you are very hungry.

Don't eat anything in between meals.

Strictly! If hungry between meals, drink water, have black tea or coffee or buttermilk or a tomato.

Walk for 45 minutes a day.

Simple enough, isn't it?

I enthusiastically set about following the new ground rules. I started with a hearty breakfast and aimed for a late lunch. The working hours were interspersed with endless cups of bitter, filter coffee. By night I was hungry but steadfastly consumed only water and black coffee. The first few days were tough but gratifying. I was operating at different places and refusing politely offered tea and biscuits and snacks under some pretext or the other. Even at home, there was some agitation. The Missus was very supportive and totally on my side and encouraged me. My Mom was troubled that I was refusing dinner and tried to coax me to have 'just a little', 'just one roti' etc. and gave me a list of ailments which occur in those who sleep hungry. My daughter was eyeing me suspiciously. What had happened to this man, who would rustle up Maggi or sandwiches at 1 a.m. and have them with gusto? Who was this stranger?

The days went by slowly.

Very slowly.

Too slowly.

Einstein probably thought about his Theory of Relativity when he was sitting and sipping water or green tea when everyone around him was enjoying a hearty meal which included his favourite foods. He would have been wondering why the time was not passing at all; and voila: The Theory of Relativity! When on a restricted diet, even the aroma of food becomes tantalizing. When you try to placate your growling stomach and try to douse the fire of hunger with water, the stomach realizes the trick after some time. But by now the kidneys are confused as to why they have to do all that extra work for no fault of theirs. And the number of trips to the washroom makes your wife wonder if you are developing prostate trouble prematurely.

Some things which had been intriguing me since the beginning of time suddenly began to make sense. Why I was repeatedly dressed up as Santa Claus in school to distribute sweets to the primary kids, why I am still the person who is always offered the menu in a restaurant by the waiter, even when we are a group of 15 people, why I was never selected for the track and field events in school and other such random occurrences. With so much realization happening suddenly, I started feeling enlightened, like The Buddha, less like Gautam Buddha and more like the Laughing Buddha. But I was nowhere near nirvana or my ideal body weight.

I was now eyeing people having food, very malevolently. The mere smell of food was now inducing varied sentiments in me. I would feel strong and Ninja-like one day for being able to avoid food. The next day there would be remorse that things had reached this stage. And on the third, there was an outright realization that I was a complete nutcase, sitting and sipping stupid, green tea while the other family members were tucking into a pizza or pastries. The fourth day would stir up a strong desire to pick up a knife and slaughter all the carrots, cucumbers and beetroots I could find. Fortunately, I did not do that because the obvious inference would have been that I had cut them up for my own consumption and would then have to eat more of the stupid stuff for the next 5 days.

To top it all, it was wedding season and I was diligently avoiding eating at most parties. There I made do with soup and if I had the necessary superpower, I would have burnt down the dessert counter just with my evil gaze. While everyone was enjoying the feast, I was chugging glass after glass of water which also necessitated frequently emptying a rapidly filling bladder. A Urologist friend noticed this, walked up and offered to operate on my prostate. My glare of contempt would have given him nightmares and I cursed him that all the spicy food on his plate would definitely give him hemorrhoids! He walked away in a huff and I felt somewhat better that someone else was also in a foul mood now.

A few times, the rules had to be relaxed. I would have a cheat snack in between, then wallow in guilt, and then have some more comfort food. Sometimes the missus would hint that she had put in a lot of effort in preparing some dish, and any married man would tell you that you don't refuse to consume that dish. Never. For no reason under the sun. Even if it means upsetting Dr Dixit or Narendra Modi. On some days, my Mom would subtly make her play; and I would again end up at the dinner table and rudely wake up my by-now lazy pancreas to start secreting insulin. On other days, I would become philosophical and ponder what was the point of working so hard if I couldn't get 2 square meals a day. Actually, I was getting 2 proper, square meals a day; what was missing were the assorted circular and triangular meals in between. But then people on a diet are better not made aware of difficult facts, lest they curse you with hemorrhoids or herpes or HIV! Yes, I know you don't believe in curses, but are you willing to risk it?

But I really needed to get my act together again, because to add insult to injury, later that night, Dr. Dixit appeared in my dreams and in his inimitable, polite tone said to me "Rehne do beta! Tum se na ho payega"!

PS: I had sent a copy of this write-up to Dr. Dixit. I am indebted to him for very gamely approving it without any edits. I am even more impressed that he took out time from his hectic schedule to appear in my dreams.

www.ingramcontent.com/pod-product-compliance
Lightning Source LLC
LaVergne TN
LVHW021141160826
845679LV00023B/1995